A New Testament Blueprint for the Church

A New Testament Blueprint for the Church

by

John Moore
and
Ken Neff

MOODY PRESS

CHICAGO

Scripture taken from the *Holy Bible: New International Version.* Copyright © 1973, 1978 by the International Bible Society. Used by permission of Zondervan Bible Publishers.

Library of Congress Cataloging in Publication Data

Moore, John, 1948–
    A New Testament blueprint for the church.
    1. Church.   2. Pastoral theology.   3. Church—
Biblical teaching.   I. Neff, Kenneth, 1943–
II. Title.
BV600.2.M646   1985   262   85-4859
ISBN 0-8024-5901-3 (pbk.)

    1 2 3 4 5 6 7 Printing/GB/Year 90 89 88 87 86 85

Printed in the United States of America

Contents

70874

To our wives,
Diane and Kay,
Who along with other brothers and sisters,
have made this book real

We would like to acknowledge with love and appreciation some who have been particularly instrumental in encouragement towards us and the content of this book. We are especially appreciate the Dallas Seminary faculty—particularly, Professors Hendricks, Ryrie, and Hodges. We also have benefited from the relationships with many in the local churches we have served with, and John has been sharpened in his relationship with the Multnomah faculty and students who have shared in his life. Finally, we would like to recognize Arthur Farstad's unpublished doctoral dissertation, *Historical and Exegetical Consideration of New Testament Church Meetings*, as an excellent treatment of certain aspects of the church. Our book is the result of exposure to many lives over a number of years, for which we are grateful.

Foreword

When we read the New Testament and relate what we read to the contemporary church, we are compelled to conclude that the relationship is more frequently one of contrast rather than comparison. Why? Why the disparity between the church of the 80s and the 1980s?

We have the same Person; we have available the same power; we are called essentially to the same purpose. But that is precisely where the rub comes. The early church never became fogged as to their purpose. They knew why they were here on earth instead of in heaven. Do you?

John Moore and Ken Neff's excellent "blueprint" seeks to answer this query in a refreshingly realistic way. Not everyone will agree with every conclusion, but that makes the book even more worthwhile. It will do more than rearrange prejudices; it will challenge presumptions.

These authors are not armchair strategists throwing rocks at the church; for years they have been deeply involved in the struggle to build a bridge between the revealed Scriptures and the daily life of a local body of believers. Along with gaining substantial academic credits, John has earned his spurs in the arena of life. Unlike many professors, he does not retreat to the comfort of the classroom to answer questions no one is asking. Ken, after finishing his seminary training, worked for a number of years on the pastoral staff of a large evangelical church. Following that, he has actively served in a number of leadership roles in the church, and has developed materials useful for rethinking and implementing biblical principles. Both men have hammered out their philosophy of ministry in a variety of forums, of which this book is a recent product.

This book is more than a vain quest for the perfect New Testament church that never did exist. Rather, it is an honest attempt to conform the church's life to the patterns of the New Testament. It is not merely descriptive, but prescriptive.

If you are tired of doing what you do in a local church without really knowing how or—more important—why, read this book. If you think your church has it "all wired," read this book and discover the divine performance code. You may need to do some changing—including changing yourself. That would be worth far more than the price of the book.

HOWARD G. HENDRICKS

Section 1

The Dilemma of Traditions, or
But We Have Always
Done It This Way

1

The Traditional Setting

BELIEVERS BIBLE FELLOWSHIP
Jeff Curtis, Pastor

February 16

Dear Pastor Mills:

Greetings from the cold southland! I still
remember our good times of sharing and encouragement
at the last pastors' conference. Yet I think I came away
with more questions than answers! I think that is good
(eventually!), but I need to get your thoughts in some
important areas.

As you know, our church has grown significantly in the last year, and we are now faced with a
series of ministry questions. They include:

1. How does a church pursue intimacy in relationships more than simply promoting a religious
   program?
2. What is the relationship of my philosophy of
   ministry to the building of a church?

3

3. How should the church view the senior pastor in relation to the other staff members? How are they both equal and yet distinct in ministry and service?
4. What are some practical suggestions for encouraging our membership in the exercise of their gifts and abilities?
5. How can I, as a pastor, fulfill my shepherding responsibilities and still be the husband and father God wants me to be?
6. How can we encourage our parents in the assembly to take an increasingly greater responsibility in the raising of their children?

I suppose I should find a seventh to make it a perfect set of questions! Even so, you can see that we are at a crossroads in ministry (and I, in life!), and we need some good biblical counsel. From my days in the community college until now, I have always valued your friendship and insights. I am again needy of that, because I want to build from a biblical blueprint.

I am looking forward to your soon reply on these important matters.

Cordially,

Jeff

—PROCLAIMING CHRIST IN OUR DAY—

Robert subconsciously flipped the corner of the letter as he again read of the concerns of his young friend and colleague. He thought back to the beginning of their friendship. It had been nine years earlier. He was in his second church at the time—now he was in his fourth—and Jeff had begun attending church while enrolled at the local community college. He remembered Jeff even then as a sincere, sober-minded young man who, even at a young age, was committed to full-time Christian service. He had taken Jeff under his "ministry wing" and given him an idea of typical experiences and questions that face a pastor in an urban American ministry. Jeff had gone on to a four-year college and seminary. He was currently in a Southern city in his first pastorate.

Yet even as Robert reread the letter one phrase kept jumping out at him. It was, "I want to build from a biblical blueprint." A biblical blueprint? What did that mean? Robert's mind raced back to the beginning of his ministry experiences in his first church—days full of encouragement and joy—meetings that began in a rented community center. Then the church had built its first building, started a Christian day school, and was currently, according to the latest report given him, trying to purchase property for a new educational and ministry complex.

A biblical blueprint? What did that mean? Robert thought of his present responsibilities. He was now the senior pastor of a large church. Current membership: more than 800. Current staff: four full-time, and four part-time. Current preaching responsibilities: two morning services, one evening service, one Monday Bible class, one Wednesday evening prayer meeting, one Thursday evening couples Bible study, and an occasional weekend ministry in nearby churches.

He was currently vice-chairman of the state committee for administration within his local denomination. Every spring he served as adjunct professor for a week at his denomination's West Coast seminary, and he was now beginning to do some biblical research on a book on church growth.

He thought about his family. His dear wife was one special woman. It seemed she was always the steady and gracious one in his life. She seemed to handle with ease the large demands of his family—two teenagers and two grade school twins—his ministry, and the expectations of the church for social and ministry responsibilities. Actually, in some ways her job was harder than his, because he was gone from home a minimum of three to four evenings a week. He wondered if he was spending enough time with his kids, but they understood how the work of the Lord was his priority. Even that thought unsettled him, but he could not put his finger on what it was that bothered him.

A biblical blueprint? Actually, the questions raised in Jeff's letter were almost precisely the ones facing him as well. His congregation had grown to about 80-percent of the capacity of the facilities. It seemed time now to build in order to provide a building that allowed for growth. Or, of course, he could begin having three Sunday morning services. He also needed to add more staff and was currently considering greater involvement and ministry through a local radio station.

But he was running out of hours in a day. There were so many opportunities, yet too little time and too few available workers. He smiled. In another fifteen years Jeff may find himself in a different yet similar ministry situation, facing the same questions of ministry and—a biblical blueprint.

Yet the more Robert thought, the more disturbed he became. More questions raced into his mind. Was it right that the pastor (or his wife) was expected at every church function? What about Paul's concern for a pastor to "manage his own household well . . . but if a man does not know how to manage his own household, how will he take care of the church of God?" (1 Tim. 3:4–5). What was the relationship of effective preaching to the increasing numbers of people who were coming to his church on Sunday mornings? He had always assumed that numerical growth was the measure of ministry success. Is that true? Is that biblical?

What about parental involvement in the training of their children? Many of the families in the church sent their children not only to Sunday school but also to private Christian day schools. Did that, at some point, do more harm than good? Did the fathers of those families still see themselves as the primary teachers of their children and wives? That same typical family, if it attended all the available church meetings during the week (which he regularly encouraged) would be exposed to twelve to fifteen different and separate instructions weekly. What did that do to the family units in his church? Did that leave the family members enough time together? Did it allow for opportunities to develop relationships in their communities?

Robert almost regretted getting the letter from his friend. He had not thought of some of those questions since his seminary days. The nature of the church, the reality of genuine spirituality, the ministry model of Christ Himself, proper conduct in the weekly meetings, leadership development, clergy and laymen responsibilities, the place of women in the church, spiritual gifts, biblical education and family involvement—these matters all related to Jeff's letter. He realized that he needed to spend some time seriously re-evaluating Jeff's questions in order to understand a biblical blueprint for himself.

Within twenty-four hours Robert found himself alone at the coast in a beach cabin. He was able to shift some ministry responsibilities, cancel some others, and after a quick trip home to pull the dozen or so books in his library that related to his questions, he had slipped away to a cabin owned by a church family. His intent was to spend a few days in private study and prayer. From that, he hoped to be able not only to answer Jeff's letter to his satisfaction but also to begin to formulate that "biblical blueprint" that he found himself now needing. Who knew—maybe it would lead to his first book!

Robert laid out the books he had brought from home. It seemed wise to peruse first what other men had written on the nature and philosophy (he wondered if the word "theology" would be better) of Christian ministry. He quickly discovered that most of the current books addressed the same basic subjects. These included:

- The purpose of the church
- The function and ministry of the church
- Qualifications and responsibilities of leaders in the church
- Classification and types of church leaders
- Spiritual gifts in the church
- Small group involvement in the church

Yet even that list bothered him a bit. He found very little, if anything, that attempted to align the nature of the spiritual life to church ministry. There was little help in the area of the relationships of leaders to the individual, family, and corporate lives of the assembly. He determined to work on those areas as well.

WHAT IS THE PURPOSE AND FUNCTION OF THE CHURCH?

Robert reviewed the materials spread out on the dining room table—as he mentally reviewed what he had been taught in seminary.

"The purpose of the church is to glorify God." The words stared back at him in a cold and lifeless way. What did that mean? He looked at the cross reference given (Eph. 1:5–6, 12):

> He predestined us to be adopted as his sons through Jesus Christ, in accordance with his pleasure and will—to the praise of his glorious grace, which he has freely given us in the One he loves. . . . in order that we, who were the first to hope in Christ, might be for the praise of his glory.

That made more sense. All that we have in God, through the grace of our Lord Jesus Christ, is ultimately to climax in our recognition and worship of Him.

As Robert reviewed books printed more recently on the subject, he found the stated purpose of the church also to be "evangelism and edification." He was hard-pressed to find a verse that *specifically* said that, but a number of verses, particularly in Acts, demonstrated the principle of spiritual and numerical growth in the spreading of the gospel. Even so, those dual purposes seemed right to him.

Yet books on philosophy of ministry and church growth varied significantly when it came to suggesting how those purposes are practically worked out in church ministry. Was the function of the church to gather to learn? Was it a training ground for ministry? Robert thought it should go further—that the church should be a place to minister, not just a training ground for ministry.

And what about spiritual gifts? It seemed there were as many opinions about spiritual gifts as there were numbers of spiritual gifts. How does a person discover his gift or gifts? What is the difference between natural ability and God-given ability? How does ministry responsibility relate to ministry giftedness? Do all pastors have a gift of teaching or preaching? He wondered about some teachers he had listened to in the past—even himself! At least two recent Christian authors had suggested that church leaders did not need spiritual gifts in order to minister. He did not understand that.

What about the gift of ruling, or management? He was not sure about himself, but he knew 1 Timothy 3:4–5 required that ability of all leaders in their homes. Yet 1 Timothy 5:17 suggested levels of management ability or activity, and proportional compensation accordingly. Robert decided management must be a ministry gift that deserved high priority.

WHAT IS THE ROLE AND RESPONSIBILITY OF LEADERS IN THE CHURCH?

Pastor Mills loved to read the latest articles and books on church leadership. In them he found guidelines for helping him in his church, as well as creative thoughts for his staff. As the senior pastor, he felt a personal responsibility to be well read in this area.

Robert's role in the church was clearly defined by the church constitution. He was the senior pastor. There was one associate pastor, one assistant pastor, and a full-time youth pastor. In decision-making, the staff pastors were to seek a consensus that, when approved by the senior pastor, was regularly taken to the congregation for vote or approval. This description made Robert feel a little like a corporate president responsible ultimately to the stockholders or employees. He liked that feeling, but he knew this was not *exactly* the New Testament description of decision-making. He could not even find the specific mention of a "trustee board" in the New Testament.

Robert remembered being challenged once in seminary by a fellow student (sometimes they asked harder questions than the professors) concerning a church constitution. Beyond the minimum document that any state requires of a church (or any non-profit corporation), what, this student asked, was the value of a constitution? Could it possibly foster an attitude of dependence on it more than study and dependence on the Scriptures? Robert had heard of churches whose expressed intent was to avoid constitutions and doctrinal statements in order to encourage their people to personal Bible study in unclear areas. Robert wondered if this was wise or whether it would *really* work.

The Scriptures speak of the pastor as a shepherd. This imagery was a picture Robert loved so well, yet at times he felt more like a cowboy than a shepherd—doing less leading and more driving. He wondered if Peter would refer to Christ as the "Chief Rancher" if 1 Peter 5:1–4 were rewritten for today. That thought sidetracked him, and he took a break to make a new pot of coffee before returning to his study.

A shepherd is one who knows his sheep. That thought made Robert a little uncomfortable. *Knowing* means different things, of course, but he did not know the names of all his members, much less their needs or life intentions. Pastoral counseling was most often crisis counseling. He had wondered a thousand times about how much less complicated some Christians' problems might have been if someone with a pastoral concern could have started helping out at the beginning of a problem rather than at the end of it.

Robert had become more curious in the last year about the subject of multiple leadership, or plurality of elders. He had done some reading on it for two reasons. First, one of the deacons in his church kept giving him articles and books to read on the subject. He suspected this would be a topic for one of the next church leadership retreats.

Second, he was curious about this "elder rule" system because it was becoming an emotionally-charged subject at various leadership meetings of his denomination. Professors at his old seminary, pastors and colleagues, and individual believers were asking increasingly difficult questions about it. Robert had voiced public concern over the ways congregations and committees seemed to be "taking sides" on the issue. Even if he wanted to change the leadership and decision-making structure of his church, Robert could not imagine how that would be accomplished.

Finally, Robert noticed a large variety of opinions on philosophy of ministry. Some men advocated the need for the local church to provide every ministry need and experience—from the regular preaching and teaching ministry to Christian schools for the child; from day care to undergraduate and graduate-level training. These men also saw only limited value in mission boards and parachurch organizations. Other men recommended a commitment to cooperation among the Christian churches and organizations planning similar ministry efforts in a similar area. From Robert's experience, the relationship between cooperation and Christian ministry sometimes better resembled the mix of oil and water. He wondered what the apostle Paul would suggest, in light of Philippians 1:15–18. But then, that was a biblical issue. He needed to stay *practical* so he could handle these questions for Jeff, and for himself.

WHAT IS THE PLACE AND MINISTRY OF BELIEVERS IN THE CHURCH?

Robert started by thinking about believers in his church. They included men and women from all kinds of occupations: bakers, plumbers, builders, pilots, teachers, secretaries. What was their place in the Body? If we found their place based on their skills, we would relate to them at the level of their physical abilities or trades. Robert had always understood them to be laymen—that is, believers in the church who are vocationally employed in professions other than the ministry. But that seemed an odd distinction, as if the work of the Lord were separated from the normal work and occupations of a believer. Yet the real ministers, Robert knew, were the full-time pastors and Christian workers. He suspected that that tradition was not biblically based, but then there does have to be some distinction between the clergy and the layman, right?

What's in a name? Reverend. Father. Pastor. Preacher. Doctor. (Robert said the last word slowly. After all, he had stayed in seminary for the purpose of being fully prepared for the ministry, and he was proud that he could display his doctoral degree on the wall of his church office.) Chaplain. Missionary. Minister. (There was that word again!) Too often, it seemed to Robert, we are known principally by our titles and jobs-of-distinction.

Robert mentally reviewed the instructions of Christ in Matthew 23, which stood as a warning against titles of distinction, in contrast to hearts committed to servanthood. Further, he remembered the end of that paragraph, which said:

The greatest among you will be your servant. For whoever exalts himself will be humbled, and whoever humbles himself will be exalted. (Matt. 23:11–12)

Does that apply to the typical approach of clergy and layman distinctions? Does that allow for distinctions based on "full-time" or layman classifications?

What about the gifted and valued contributions of each member of the body? Robert readily admitted to himself that the church ministry had become rather professional in the last ten to fifteen years. When a staff need exists, a personnel search is made for the most capable candidate—usually one who is a stranger to the congregation in need. Very rarely had Robert seen, or heard of, a believer who had been proved in his own congregation and prepared for a place of service to the assembly. That certainly seemed to be the pattern of Acts 6, as well as the recommendation of 1 Timothy 3:10. But it was hard to imagine its actually happening in a church.

What about foreign missions in the church? The usual practice was for a missionary candidate to travel around and gather support from many churches before he or she would leave for the field. Yet most of the missionaries that Robert's church supported were virtual strangers to the congregation, particularly to the newer members. The proving process for these candidates rarely involved an extended stay at any one congregation. Robert wondered about that in light of Paul and Barnabas and their relationship to the church at Antioch.

The inquiring seminary student also had once asked him about the "theological justification" for boarding schools for missionaries' children—schools that separated the children from their parents. Admittedly, it did seem to go against the pattern of the home's being a proving ground for ministry qualifications, but it all seemed in the most worthwhile of causes, inasmuch as the parents were ministering in the cause of Christ. Jim, his fellow student, had wondered if there might be workable alternative, one that would also comply with the biblical concerns. Robert decided to study that more later.

Related to Robert's thoughts on professionalism and the ministry was a cross reference he noticed in one of the books he was reading. It was 1 Corinthians 14:26. That text suggested that in the New Testament church there was a regular commitment to an "open" meeting—that believers came to those meetings ready to participate in the edification and encouragement of the saints. Apart from the aspect of the question that related to tongues-speaking and prophecy, Robert wondered how such a principle could be incorporated into an audience of 400. He admitted (again to himself) that most believers come to the Sunday meeting ready to "be ministered to." There were few opportunities, if any, to minister to the gathered church in an open fashion. The logistics and possible problems of changing to a mutual edification style of meeting made Robert shudder.

Robert glanced outside and noticed that it was dark. In his interest and concern over these ministry questions, he had gone right past both lunch and dinner. Yet Robert believed he now had the beginnings of some answers that would aid Jeff in his current situation—and would then begin to answer his own similar, unsettling questions.

But the letter would have to wait until tomorrow. Right now he was most interested in finding a hamburger.

2

Typical Solutions to Traditional Problems

February 23

Dear Brother Jeff,

It does not seem like two months have already passed since we last fellowshipped together at the pastors' conference. It was good to get your letter, which updated me on happenings at your church. It was also hard getting your letter! I thought I taught you never to ask questions that I had trouble answering! Seriously, your letter prompted some "soul searching" on my part, a brief study on some of the questions you raised, and now hopefully some fresh answers from a "biblical blueprint."

I would like to answer some of your questions in the order that I studied them. I hope this provides a context in which we can continue to dialogue the issues together.

First, I appreciated very much your questions on a philosophy, or theology, of ministry. It seems to me that the overall purpose of the church is to glorify Christ. He is the Head of the church – and the focus and goal as well.

Even as He is the Head, we are given the "day to day" responsibilities, as pastors, of managing His people. Therefore, it would seem to me that the church should be, before the world, a picture of the excellence of our Lord. To me, that means that both our programs and facilities for ministry should be first class! I suppose the model and instructions concerning the Tabernacle in Exodus could serve as an example. God is a God of excellence, and we should be a reflection of Him.

I share your concerns and questions regarding program and staff development. I remember your sharing with me the quality of some of the young men and women in your church, and what able leaders you think they will someday make. But what if they do not have the professional skills of someone outside the church? Should the church suffer because of some "in-house" principle? I think not. Rather . . .

Jeff's mind drifted from the letter in his hands to the lives of some of the brothers and sisters in his church. A small twinge of disappointment slipped past his heart. He thought of two of the young men—men who desired greater responsibility in the church. They were full of enthusiasm for the labor of the ministry. They also were full of questions. Did God want them to stay in this city, develop an occupation or trade, and continue to minister in the church? Or was it better to leave the church and go to the seminary for training, with the hope of sometime being relocated in this or another church that needed their ministry skills?

Jeff was not sure why he felt disappointed. Maybe it was just that he had come to love those men, and he would miss their presence and fellowship. It did seem right to get the best possible training for the ministry. But what would happen in the meantime? Could the church afford to wait for those men to return? Would staff need to be chosen from another area?

Jeff had recently taught through the book of Acts, and a phrase in Acts 6 continued to drift through his mind: "Choose seven men from among you who are known" (6:3). Coupled with this thought was the still-fresh experience of a sister church in the community. The members had brought in a pastor after a long weekend of examination and prayer. As it turned out, the church did not realize that this man had serious marital and business problems. The whole situation had ended in a community scandal of immorality and embezzlement. Jeff had tried to help in the healing process of some of the church members. But some of the believers, now six months later, had still not recovered spiritually.

Jeff supposed that the church deserved the most skilled pastors available. Yet he still had serious questions about this attitude of "professionalism and excellence." He enjoyed the meetings in his church that were handled with skill. Nevertheless, there was a sense of informality and personal commitment in the church in Acts that he had seen repeatedly in his study. For example, a principle and regular focus of the New Testament church was the proclamation of Christ around the Lord's Table (Acts 2:42, 46; 20:7). The practice in his church, and in the churches he was most familiar with, placed the Table at the end of the morning service, usually on a monthly basis. Somehow it seemed the practice came short of the New Testament model—particularly with the habits of "clock-watching" that that practice encouraged.

Should the world be impressed with the church? Should church buildings be community illustrations of "excellence"? Should that signal to the unbeliever that God is "alive and well" among them? Jeff had enjoyed the words of Christ in Matthew 22. As an essential summary of the whole Old Testament, Christ had reminded His critics that to "love your neighbor as yourself" (22:39) was the second commandment, and like the first. "All the Law and the Prophets hang on these two commandments" (22:40). That taught that the essentials of the saint's life-style were a commitment to love—first, to loving the Lord, and second, to loving those around us. How did that fit with the witness of brick and mortar? Could buildings of flesh and blood do better? It would be nice if it were biblically so. Jeff imagined that it would be economically so.

The thought of credibility raced through Jeff's mind. To both the believing and unbelieving community, a church has credentials in two basic ways: first, by its building or facilities, and second, by the pastor. Jeff thought back to an embarrassing conversation of the preceding week. He had been considering the nature of the Body of Christ, with particular interest in the fact of Christ as Head. A visitor came into the church (building) and introduced himself, and then said, "Well, pastor, tell me about *your* church." With not the slightest intent of embarrassing his guest, Jeff had replied, "Oh, you mean *Christ's* church!" The visitor quickly amended his questions, but the conversation ended in both men being embarrassed by the conversation.

Jeff had not intended that; he had just voiced what had been his concern of study recently. He still thought he was *right* in what he said, but he regretted the embarrassment of the moment. Jeff thought of Paul's charge to the Ephesian elders: "Be shepherds of the Church of God, which he bought with his own blood" (Acts 20:28*b*). The church certainly did not belong to any man, or pastor. It belonged to Christ, who was its Head.

> principle? I think not. Rather, it seems that God's people deserve the best that we can offer in clergy and ministry-skills.
>
> Second, and related to the first, you asked concerning the development of the gifts and abilities of believers in your church. I have some exciting news for you! I just recently discovered a Spiritual Gifts Inventory Questionnaire (SGIQ) that takes a layman through a series of questions which guarantees him the discovery of at least one of his spiritual gifts! Can you imagine how . . .

For a second time in the reading of the letter from his friend and mentor, Jeff's heart slipped a notch in disappointment. He had hoped that Dr. Mills would do better on this question. He remembered one extended conversation they had had at the pastors' conference. It was Jeff's growing suspicion that the questions of spiritual gifts had been seriously mistaken in current ministry terms. Indeed, there were multiple opportunities for seminars, questionnaires, and books on "how to discover and use your spiritual gift(s)." But the New Testament perspective seemed to be not so much the discovering of one's spiritual gift(s) as the proper use of one's gift(s). There were no easy discovery formulas in Jeff's study of the question in the New Testament. He suspected the apostle Paul would have been more than a little bit amused at the current state of the church in relation to spiritual gifts. Yet if the essential New Testament instructions were pointed more to proper use than discovery, how did that work in the church? Were there contexts in which the gifts and ministries could be developed? Could a greater emphasis on small group and regular home meetings help here? Jeff suspected he had little remaining interest for the SGIQ.

> how much a church can be benefited if it mobilizes its laity with each member knowing and using his or her gift!
>
> Third, in the area of leadership, I am going to confide some things to you that need to stay confidential until I have time to work them through with my staff and church (which could be years). I need to share these things with you, but they must not go beyond you.
>
> I think our church is not working from a proper enough "biblical blueprint" currently in matters of leadership and decision-making. As you might remember, we have a deacon board, a trustee board, and ultimately congregational approval of major program changes and financial expenditures. That pattern has worked relatively well, and it certainly seems to fit the "democratic" model within America.
>
> But I am suspicious that we could do better! I would like to move more to a system of having an elder board, a deacon board, and some kind of congregational involvement in the decision-making without seeing them as the ultimate authority in the church. This has implications for how we see our church constitution, the future of my denomination, and even the relationship between our churches and our Bible schools and seminaries!
>
> I would like to see the church staff as elders in the body. I would still need to be the "senior pastor" (or whatever we decide to call it!) since the church still needs someone who is in charge, and who provides direction for the church. But I would like more of a team spirit! I think this will make my staff feel more like part of the team. It seems that . . .

Jeff gripped the pages of the letter with excitement. He had no idea his former pastor was considering those concepts. He was greatly encouraged. He knew it would take courage for Robert to pursue that line of thinking within his denomination. But that was almost exactly where Jeff had come in his own study.

It was readily apparent to Jeff that the New Testament church leaders were called overseers, or elders. They were together able to shepherd and guard the flock of God. It seemed to Jeff that a few strategic New Testament passages affirmed the plurality of this leadership team in a singular church context—that is, a plurality of elders in each local assembly. Jeff had not seen or heard of much concerning that concept, but he was committed to seeing it become a working reality in his church.

Even so, many questions remained in Jeff's mind. What was his place of distinction in the church? Was that even a proper consideration? Christ seemingly distinguished Peter in relation to the twelve, but he also instructed the whole group carefully in matters of servanthood and humility. How did that all fit together?

What were the implications of those things for the financial support needed for one who served in full-time ministry (actually, Jeff had tried to begin using the phrase *vocational ministry*, since it seemed to him that all Christians were "full time"). Jeff understood, like Robert, that he still needed to provide the leadership for the elder team. All groups look for, and need, a leader—or so he had always been taught. But would the elders be distinguished by their educational degrees? By their skill in ministry? By their ministry tasks? And, if so, who would make the decisions that provided those distinctions and the appropriate financial compensations? It certainly was true that Jeff was coming up with more questions than answers these days.

Further, what was the congregation's role in decision making? Although Robert's church had "congregational rule," Jeff's had been established along lines of "elder rule." At times it seemed that both were extremes of what the New Testament recommended. Congregational rule seemed to allow for church members' taking authority that superseded the biblical model. Yet Jeff had to admit that in his "elder rule" situation the congregation was less informed and less involved than he would like. He suspected that his situation was closer to the biblical model. In that he agreed with him. But did he have the letter and spirit of the New Testament on this question? He determined to spend more time studying Acts 6.

Another implication of this issue was the relationship of the church with Bible schools or seminaries. If the church determined that the qualifications of 1 Timothy 3 were essential for ministry, then that would mean men who graduated from those schools *might not necessarily be ready* for vocational Christian ministry. Would those schools agree with that?

What about the place of women in the church? Jeff's church had a number of very capable women who were greatly interested, and well-read, on the subject of ministry. Many had attended available seminars and Bible study groups on the subject. What was their place? What did Paul's warning "I do not permit a woman to teach or have authority over a man" mean (1 Tim. 2:12)? How did that apply? Was there a place for church staff positions for women in the church? Was the distinguishing issue ability or ministry-skill? Jeff knew intrinsically that that was not the issue. He only had to think of the gracious stability and character of his own wife to know that. In addition, he had often found himself feeling inadequate in counseling women in matters of home and marriage. He just could not empathize with them as another woman could. He wondered if the Scriptures would reinforce that feeling. Indeed, Robert was right. These were important areas.

> my staff feel more like part of the team. It seems that the church-at-large, the body of Christ, is ready for this change. I hope our local church is!
>
> Fourth, the last area you mentioned in your letter has caused me, in some sense, the greatest concern and re-evaluation. It is the area of the home. There is no area that I commit more regularly to the Lord in prayer than my home.
>
> It seems that the home provides a context for both qualification for the ministry and an illustration of commitment to the Lord and to His work. It is true that Paul considers the home – that is, relationships to a wife and children – to be principal considerations for qualification for ministry for an overseer or elder (1 Tim. 3). But it seems also that a commitment to the Lord as first in your life means that the priority of Christian ministry is even greater than the priority to the home. Now I would be the first to say that I want to do the best in both of those areas! Yet, hasn't it been the history of the church that dedicated men and women have left all to follow Christ? Aren't missionaries who

use boarding schools for their children an excellent
example of this kind of godly commitment?

Likewise, we live in a modern age where fathers
(and in increasing numbers, mothers) do not stay home
with their children. They go to their jobs. Children go
to school. In our busy, modern day it seems prudent to
enlist the most capable teachers to train up our children
in both Sunday school and in their day school experiences. It seems the church is responsible for taking up
the slack caused by the reduced availability of the modern
Christian parent. Thus, while I would prefer seeing the
father and parents taking primary responsibility for the
training of their families, it seems this is impractical in
our day. I will continue to study this subject.

Let me say again how glad I was to hear from you!
I love you as a brother, and always look forward to sharing in your life. Write again soon!

> Committed with you to the
> success of the church,
>
> Pastor Robert

Jeff placed the letter from Robert on his desk and stared for a
long time out his window. This last area was also, in some senses,
the closest to his heart. He and his wife had not yet been blessed
with children. Frankly, he wondered where they would get time to
rear them. He too was often out three or four evenings every
week. A typical work week involved sixty hours or more of his
time. Many days began with early morning meetings and ended
with late nights in the homes of his church families. He wondered
what his wife would say about this fourth area in Robert's letter.
Would she share Robert's enthusiasm and commitment to the
ministry—even over the family?

How does a first priority to the Lord size up with competing
priorities for work and family? Do we live in a modern age in
which the principal role of the parent is assumed by the church?
What do our children think of that? What principles offer the best
working model for the long-term health of the church?

Jeff glanced at the clock. He was late for an appointment with a
real estate agent who had a church building for sale. As he left his

office, he remembered his original concerns in his letter to Dr. Mills. He had said that he wanted to build from a biblical blueprint. He certainly was convinced that that determination left a person with more questions than answers. He suspected he knew something of the questions. Now, if he could just begin to come up with some answers.

Section 2

The Biblical Alternative for Church Ministry, or When All Else Fails, Read the Bible

3

Character and Conduct of the Church

The questions raised by Pastors Robert and Jeff in the first two chapters are all too typical. In fact, their questions cover the essential gamut of debate in areas of study on the church today. Their questions are not "cloistered in ivory towers." They are grounded in the genuine concerns of making the church all that God intended it to be. Their motives as well as their questions are good. Where they both fell short, Robert more than Jeff, was in the thing that concerned them most: a biblical blueprint. What is it? What is the relation of Christian ministry, as seen in the New Testament, to the church? What is the form and function of a church that genuinely desires its leadership, organization, relationships, and families to be grounded in the eternal truths of Scripture? It is to the description of that form and function that the remainder of this book is pointed.

CHARACTER OF THE CHURCH

Multiple instructions and guidelines have been given concerning the character and nature of the church. Like barkers along the carnival midway, different teachers call from their booths—all with different offers. One will say, "The church exists to give glory to God." Another will add, "The church exists to perform the dual roles of evangelism and edification." From still others we hear, "The church is the church only when it exists for others." Even without climbing on any of this carnival's nerve-wrenching rides, one can come away dizzy and disoriented as he seeks answers for the form and function of the church. And certainly not last, from a larger corner booth we hear, "The church is realizing its true nature when you are able to worship 'with your kind of people.'" Truth is found in sameness rather than oneness.

It is not surprising that the saint who wanders through this carnival of values and opinions has little bearing left for deciding where are the biblical spots for driving "the tent peg of ministry." What guidelines are to be trusted for finding biblical bases? Vital to this overall question is the primary necessity of asking what the church *is* before we ask what the church is to *do*.

THE NATURE OF THE CHURCH

Conduct your own informal survey. Ask a few people what they think of when you say the word "church." Odds are that four out of five, maybe nine out of ten, will speak in terms of buildings and programs. This easily illustrates how much our American culture resists a rethinking of the nature of the church. And yet the Scripture will insist that the church is "you who pray, not where you pray." The New Testament church is made of flesh and blood, not brick and mortar.

Ephesians 3:6

> This mystery is that through the gospel the Gentiles are heirs together with Israel, members together of one body, and sharers together in the promise in Christ Jesus.

The apostle Paul was a minister with a unique message, called a "mystery," which was revealed by God to him and the other apostles (3:5). This mystery was something unthinkable to the traditional and devout Jew. It was that the Jew and the Gentile were one. One body. Joint-heirs.

Gentiles are heirs together with Israel. The gospel of God had produced a remarkable unity. That heritage was rooted in those believers' reception of the gospel and the gracious deposit of the Holy Spirit as a guarantee of their final redemption (1:13–14; cf.

1:18–19a). As well, there was now in Christ no middle wall of partition—no hostility—for those who were saved by grace (2:14). Christ was the end of the law. Until now Israel had had strict legislation that separated her from her Gentile neighbors, and Paul was saying, "Enough!" Indeed, the ground at the base of the cross was level.

Members together of one body. This unity or oneness reached to the imagery of a human body. Now both Jew and non-Jew were intimately joined in one spiritual body. The incredible thought of this spiritual merger must have been almost unthinkable to the orthodox Jew. Oil and water. That described the Jew and the Gentile. Yet here was revelation from God through Paul that these groups were joined together as co-members of one single Body. Just as it was physically impossible to divide a human body without detrimental effects, even so any conception of division or distinction between Jew and Gentile did serious harm to the work of the gospel.

Sharers together in the promise of Christ Jesus. Furthermore, all the majesty and authority of the law of Moses, the prophets, and the Psalms climaxed in the blessings of salvation in the Lord Jesus and in the reality of being co-owners of those promises. The devout Jew had always understood the primacy of Israel for the revelation and blessings of God. This understanding came from the biblical covenant with Abraham, Isaac, and Jacob (Gen. 12, 15). Now the grace of the Lord Jesus had extended equally to the Gentile world. The impact of this on the Jew was illustrated by Peter's repeated struggle with these concepts (Acts 10:19–23; Gal. 2:11–21).

Colossians 3:11

> Here there is no Greek or Jew, circumcised or uncircumcised, barbarian, Scythian, slave or free, but Christ is all, and is in all.

To the New Testament authors the Body of Christ was "paradise regained." The restoration process was done at conversion (3:3). Now the life of all believers is "hidden with Christ in God." There is no distinction.

Distinctions were a specialized activity and concern in Christ's day. There were divisions based on nationality or creed, on family background or spiritual heritage, and on the social or economic status of a person. But in Christ "there is no ... " distinction or division. This is the essence of the Body of Christ. Any thinking or system that begins to encourage distinction based on "earthly" standards misses the heart of the gospel impact on believers.

Strategically, it is from that very theological base that Paul then appeals to us to receive, bear with, and forgive one another "as the Lord forgave you." This behavior, bound together by love, will lead to the outworking of unity (3:12–14).

Galatians 3:28

> There is neither Jew nor Greek, slave nor free, male nor female, for you are all one in Christ Jesus.

In his epistle to the Galatians, Paul had also reminded his readers that this "distinctionless" body was also "neither slave nor free, male nor female." Again the composite of the Body of Christ is strategic to Paul's understanding of what believers are to understand about themselves and their mission in the world. In other words, if the body is functioning as it should in local assemblies, individual members will have no apprehension concerning their worth in terms of financial status, work circumstances, or even gender. Because of who they are in Christ, neither a slave nor a blue-collar worker nor a woman need feel any "lesser status" within the body. Of course, ministry tasks and responsibilities may differ (cf. 1 Tim. 2–3; Tit. 1–2), but as brothers and sisters together, clothed in the righteousness of Christ, and as co-laborers in the body, there is no distinction. This teaching was vital to the New Testament church.

UNITY, NOT DISTINCTION!

One of the basic skills many of us picked up as children was the ability to major in the minors. Whether it was in comparisons of Christmas presents, the number of peas or green beans on the plate, or "who-stayed-up-the-latest-last-night," we specialized in matters of distinction, not unity. Yet the opposite is stressed in the New Testament, and the opposite is to be true of New Testament saints.

Acts 15:7b–11

> Brothers, you know that some time ago God made a choice among you that the Gentiles might hear from my lips the message of the gospel and believe. God, who knows the heart, showed that he accepted them by giving the Holy Spirit to them, just as he did to us. He made no distinction between us and them, for he purified their hearts by faith. Now then, why do you try to test God by putting on the necks of the disciples a yoke that neither we nor our fathers have been able to bear? No! We believe it is through the grace of our Lord Jesus that we are saved, just as they are.

In the Jerusalem Council the apostles and elders came together to consider the challenge of the false teachers concerning the addition of circumcision and the law of Moses to the work of the Spirit in the Body of Christ. This was no small threat, for in it was the distortion of the very gospel of God. It is a delight to see the apostle Peter step to the forefront in the controversy. Peter, who had struggled with this whole knotty issue himself (cf. Acts 10; Gal. 2), now spoke on behalf of the Gentiles. Of interest to us is Peter's emphasis on two things.

God made no distinction between Jew and Gentile, for he purified their hearts by faith. After Peter's struggles with the vision of the sheet (Acts 10) and the favoritism exhibited in the assembly at Jerusalem, following a visit from James (Gal. 2:11–13), he addressed the Council with the enthusiasm and clarity that came from the lessons he had learned. Peter had come to grips with the reality and character of the Body of Christ. He realized God's greatest concern was, and is, the heart (Acts 15:8a). The tool of distinctionism had really become the lathe of legalism— merely an excuse for cutting and dividing according to arbitrary and external biases.

In matters of the inner man or the spiritual plight of a man without the Savior, God's concern is for the heart. When the heart was right with God, then there was no continuing distinction. It is hardly surprising that there is no distinction in Christ. To consider a bias for one group of believers or another is to bring defect to the holy and complete work of salvation (cf. Rom. 3:22).

It is through the grace of our Lord Jesus that we are saved, just as those in the New Testament church were. Additionally, based on the reality of a distinctionless salvation in Christ, Peter gave the faithful saying of the apostles and the Council concerning

salvation. It is the work of grace that leads to salvation (Eph.
2:8–10). The important phrase "just as they are" in the Acts
passage settles the issue. It proclaims equality of spiritual heritage
and benefit to both Jew and Gentile. Peter's ability to understand
this revelation from God became the platform for his understanding of the issues that threatened the church. Would to God that
the church of our day could lay issues of doctrine and controversy on the "conciliar table" for biblical evaluation.

1 Corinthians 3:21–23

> So then, no more boasting about men! All things are yours, whether
> Paul or Apollos or Cephas or the world or life or death or the present or
> the future—all are yours, and you are of Christ, and Christ is of God.

The church at Corinth faced many unique challenges. As an
assembly, it had an abundance of spiritual gifts exhibited in the lives
of the members (1:7). They were benefactors of an extended and
godly ministry given to them by the apostle Paul, who served in
humility and wisdom (2:1–5). Yet there were divisions and factions
among them (1:10–12). Paul develops the first section of his epistle
along lines of concern and instruction concerning those matters.

Rather than boasting about the ministries and abilities of man,
be they Peter, Paul, or Apollos, the Corinthians were to retrench
according to the reality of their true possessions and characteristics
in Christ. These believers had been abundantly blessed. All the
servants of God who had ministered to them belonged to them.
All matters of time or possessions, things present or things to
come, belonged to them corporately. Why? Because "you are of
Christ, and Christ is of God."

UNITY, NOT STATUS

One of the more amusing times of the academic year for John is
commencement. In one sense it is certainly a time of joy and
encouragement as hundreds of men and women fulfill a curricular
regime and move on into fields of service and further study. Yet,
for John, it is also amusing.

Here he is in an incredibly ridiculous robe—with a multicol-
ored hood that threatens to restrict his windpipe, sleeves that he
could use to store his lunch, and a cap that has absolutely no
utility short of supporting a tassel that keeps dislodging his

contacts. Further, many things about the ceremony—the academic credentials, the clothing, the separated seating—wear away at the careful truths of the New Testament concerning relationships with others in the Body of Christ. Maybe a commencement address on the brotherhood of believers would help.

Matthew 23:8–12

> But you are not to be called "Rabbi," for you have only one Master and you are all brothers. And do not call anyone on earth "father," for you have one Father, and he is in heaven. Nor are you to be called "teacher," for you have one Teacher, the Christ. The greatest among you will be your servant. For whoever exalts himself will be humbled, and whoever humbles himself will be exalted.

If there remained any doubt concerning the essential character of the church as a community of brothers and sisters redeemed and now seen as "one in Christ Jesus" (Gal. 3:28d), a brief reminder of our Lord's words to His disciples settles the matter. In the context of both defining true greatness in the kingdom (Matt. 23:11–12; cf. 20:20–28) and contrasting that servant model with the conduct of the religious leaders of His day, Christ reaffirmed the unity and oneness that composes the soil for the true roots of the kingdom.

For you have only one Master, and you are all brothers. In keeping with the honor and prestige, not to mention the tassels and thrones reserved for the members of the Sanhedrin, the disciples deferred to the customs and thoughts of their day by attaching titles of esteem to those who were the teachers of the law. Christ took issue with that practice and said rather that the disciples were to look at no disciple as greater than another. They were all equally brothers, and commonly looked to the one Master, their Father in heaven. This emphasis provides the backdrop for the church's leadership model.

James 2:1–5

> My brothers, as believers in our glorious Lord Jesus Christ, don't show favoritism. Suppose a man comes into your meeting wearing a gold ring and fine clothes, and a poor man in shabby clothes also comes in. If you show special attention to the man wearing fine clothes and say, "Here's a good seat for you," but say to the poor man, "You

stand there," or, "Sit on the floor by my feet," have you not discriminated among yourselves and become judges with evil thoughts? Listen, my dear brothers: Has not God chosen those who are poor in the eyes of the world to be rich in faith and to inherit the kingdom he promised those who love him?

If Matthew 23 describes those who are thinking "too highly" of themselves, James 2 describes those who are thinking "too lowly" of others. James and the Spirit of God move quickly to essential issues and inconsistencies in the early church—matters that need careful definition in order to continue God's work among the young community of believers.

The inconsistency of favoritism brought a quick response from James. James's immediate audience was showing preferential treatment of the rich over the poor in the local assembly. Such behavior, James states, is entirely inappropriate from a number of perspectives. First, it is a misunderstanding of the frailty and temporary nature of wealth (1:9–11). Second, it betrays personal judgments motivated by evil intent (2:4). Third, and most significant, it misses the essential work that poorness, or difficult circumstances, has in the life of the believer (2:5; cf. 1:2–4).

Yet woven skillfully through this theological tapestry are the important threads concerning equality within the Body of Christ. (James does refer to his readers repeatedly as "brothers and sisters" [1:2, 9, 16, 19; 2:1, 5, 14–15].) Further, James reminds his readers that in judging their poor brethren they were sinfully demanding a legal standard of perfection (2:8–11).

But most significant, to promote any feature of favoritism among the assembly was to deny the truth of their own salvation. James states that their heavenly Father, who is generous to all (1:5) and does not change (1:17) chose "to give us birth through the word of truth, that we might be a kind of firstfruits of all He created" (1:18). The point to the readers was unmistakable. It was God who gave grace abundantly and *evenly* to all the saints. His grace to them, as well as to James himself, was to result in their being held up *together* to the Lord as firstfruit from His harvest (cf. Deut. 26:1–11; 1 Cor. 15:20–23).

CONDUCT OF THE CHURCH

The now famous Lucy and Linus, from the children's cartoon strip *Peanuts*, are gazing out their window, watching the rain pour down. With a deep sigh, Lucy laments, "Boy, look at it rain. What if it floods the whole world?"

Linus quickly responds, "It will never do that. In the ninth chapter of Genesis God promised Noah that it would never happen again, and the sign of the promise is the rainbow."

"You've taken a great load off my mind," Lucy replies. To which Linus responds, "Sound theology has a way of doing that!" Similarly, sound theology in the church—understanding who we actually are in Christ's Body—brings theological relief in relation to questions of what we are to do in the church. Ephesians 4 contains one of the classic blueprints for ministry in the New Testament.

Character leads to conduct. Relationship leads to responsibility. Doctrine leads to duty. So it is in Ephesians 4:1–16. That passage presents the flesh and blood of New Testament ministry in the church. It is a picture of body growth and of the unique and supernatural nurture of lives in the supportive and cooperative atmosphere of a local assembly. It is divided into three paragraphs. Each contributes a key feature of the ministry and leads to the following concepts.

THE COMMITMENT OF UNITY (4:1–6)

Building on the established truths of Ephesians 3:6, the apostle now reaffirms the intimate relationship between who we are and what we do. Believers are one, not only through the grace of the Lord Jesus Christ but also because this essential unity is seen in the very character of God Himself.

> There is one body and one Spirit—just as you were called to one hope when you were called—one Lord, one faith, one baptism; one God and Father of all, who is over all and through all and in all. (Eph. 4:4–6)

In rereading all of Paul's epistles, one can find that subject of unity mentioned more often than any other. It is time for candid acknowledgement of this in the Christian church.

It is hardly wavering toward liberalism to reaffirm the preoccupation of God the Spirit and the apostle Paul concerning the character and conduct of the Body of Christ. Such an emphasis is foundational to Pauline theology.

Second, the very source and substance of our salvation, God

Himself, is infinitely more interested in our understanding the concept of unity in the body than we are. Cultivating "the unity of the Spirit through the bond of peace" (4:3) is exactly consistent with the God we love and serve.

Third, unity is not automatic. This may seem readily apparent, yet Paul made a special point of reminding the Ephesians that they were "to make every effort" in pursuing these objectives of unity and peace in the assembly. These words paint a picture of a miner who is laboring hard in his work for the reward of small but valuable gems. In the same way, the believer who labors hard in the work of unity is commended by God.

THE CONTRIBUTION OF DIVERSITY (4:7–10)

Paul continues in precisely the same way as the chapter began. He reaffirms the truth of our salvation that we are benefactors of grace by God's grace and initiative. Earlier Paul had written that we were to live "worthy of the calling you have received" (4:1). Now he states that "to each of us grace has been given as Christ apportioned it" (4:7). Whatever our ministry opportunities or abilities, they are no cause for boasting as if we have influenced the portion of grace God has given us.

The grace ministry of Christ has brought gifts and distributions to the church. The foundation of the structure has already been laid:

> Consequently, you are . . . members of God's household, built on the foundation of the apostles and prophets, with Christ Jesus himself as the chief cornerstone. (Eph. 2:19–20)

This diversity of gifts and the careful understanding and exercise of them complements the unity of the body. The commitment to unity is a sameness that keeps members of the body as a unit during growth and maturing pains, and their unique exercise of gifts complements and encourages the body in a multifaceted way equal to the various needs and interests of any local assembly. Here we see unity in purpose and diversity in function.

THE CONDUCT OF BRINGING BELIEVERS TO MATURITY (4:11–16)

The church as a living organism is alive and vitally rooted in the grace of Christ. But a ministry dilemma remains. The church exists, both corporately and individually, in immature form. It is made up of young believers who need to profit from the lives of other saints for the mutual growth of the body. The real labor of the ministry is seen in this passage. There can be no more worthy purpose for the believer than the investing of his life in the lives of others to bring them to maturity. All structures and philosophies of ministry come back to this watershed passage, and others like it, which insist on spiritual maturity as the goal for our work and life together.

As before, we can see three vital emphases in this passage. First, the reason God has given a diversity of grace-gifts to the Body is so that God's people can be prepared for works of service and that the Body of Christ may be corporately built up to the unity and maturity that reflects the fullness of Christ.

> To prepare God's people for works of service, so that the body of Christ may be built up until we all reach unity in the faith and in the knowledge of the Son of God and become mature, attaining to the whole measure of the fullness of Christ. (Eph. 4:12–13)

As one old saint once said, "It's amazin' what you can learn about the Bible by just reading it!" The Scriptures are patently clear. The work of the ministry is people—people who labor at the long-range goals of seeing brothers and sisters established in good works (which is to be the result of our salvation (cf. Eph. 2:10) and in unity and maturity within the Body of Christ.

But what is the structure of this corporate unity? There is no greater unity than "the whole measure of the fullness of Christ," based on a mature understanding of doctrine. There is no reason to be hesitant about doctrine. The greatest sources of unity in the body come at the doctrinal level (cf. Acts 2:42). But it is equally true that mere doctrine is not the end goal—people are. The umbrella of acceptance in the body must go beyond doctrinal precision.

Two passages illustrate this life-changing truth about the place of doctrine. In that remarkable little thank-you note for contributions from the saints, Paul writes:

> It is true that some preach Christ out of envy and rivalry . . . out of selfish ambition . . . supposing that they can stir up trouble for me. . . . The important thing is that in every way, whether from false motives or true, Christ is preached. (Phil. 1:15–18)

Notice how Paul refused to speak words of condemnation or judgment against believers who he knew were ministering out of motives not strictly Christ-centered. He allowed no negative ministry-motives to deter him from his joy and delight in the work of the gospel.

The second passage is equally remarkable:

> All of us who are mature should take such a view of things. And if on some point you think differently, that too God will make clear to you. (Phil. 3:15).

Paul now backs away from the heavy-handed approach to convincing others of his (and God's) point of view. Rather, he allows for the process of maturity to be finished in the lives of saints who may disagree (with this revelation), and he expects that in God's timing those truths will be established in them. In matters both of ministry motives and doctrinal precision, relationships in the body come first.

Second, the entire pattern is one that sees the individual believer progressing from infancy to adulthood.

> Then we will no longer be infants, tossed back and forth by the waves, and blown here and there by every wind of teaching and by the cunning and craftiness of men in their deceitful scheming. Instead, speaking the truth in love, we will in all things grow up into him who is the Head, that is, Christ. (Eph. 4:14–15)

Immaturity is characterized by doctrinal vacillation. Maturity is characterized by one whose growth and life is increasingly "into him who is the Head." But how? Notice the critical phrase at the beginning of 4:15. In our English text it reads, "Speaking the truth in love." It can be literally rendered "Truthing in love." This refers to the individual parts of the Body of Christ who commit themselves to a dual ministry. Truth without love leads to harshness, and love without truth leads to an absence of standards. The whole of Christian ministry in the New Testament is summarized in the phrase "Indeed, even Christ Himself is the fullness of grace and truth" (John 1:16–17). In other words, the responsibility of growth in the body rests squarely on the shoulders of believers who commit themselves to this "truthing in love" in life and relationships.

Paul selected his words carefully here. The seedplot for body growth is the loving, gentle, nurturing of love (*agape*) on the ground of doctrinal truth. Rather than using *phileo*, which means brotherly affection, or *stergo*, which means mutual respect, or *eros*, which means principally craving or physical desire, Paul used *agape* to represent what love is. This word has been carefully used in Ephesians:

1:4   The electing love of God that selected us as saints in eternity past
2:4   The merciful, gracious love of God that granted us salvation while we were spiritually dead
3:17–18 The dimensionless wealth of the love of Christ bringing us to the fullness of God

Now, in 4:15 this love (*agape*), modeled by Christ, is defined as "the generous choosing of the interest of another over oneself." It is the determined decision to seek the interests of others who are regarded as brothers and sisters in the faith. We are "rooted and established in love" (3:17; cf. 1 Tim. 1:5). Nurture and growth for a believer happens when love and truth are coupled carefully in one life and then in many lives in the church, so that the whole body will "grow up into him who is the Head, that is, Christ" (4:15*b*). Then the promise of body growth and the proper working of each part will be accomplished.

Our third observation about these texts continues this point most forcefully:

> From him the whole body, joined and held together by every supporting ligament, grows and builds itself up in love, as each part does its work. (4:16)

As each believer labors personally in areas of truth and love, the text promises that Christ Himself will coordinate those parts into a whole that is cooperative, co-supportive, and expressed by love. Now we see that not only does each believer do his part, but that edification and growth in the body can be accomplished only when the body is working together. In our individualized Western society, this concept is a splash of cold water. Essentially then, our unity in God Himself, coupled with the diverse abilities within the body, is in final composite form, to resemble a body—fitted and formed by all its parts working together (held together by the glue of maturity) and clothed in the attribute of love. This imagery speaks forcefully and magnificently to the issue of the proper conduct of the church in our day.

CONCLUSIONS

In each paragraph of this important scripture section on Christian ministry, a principle is given that leads to a promise.

	PRINCIPLE	PROMISE
Eph. 4:1–6	Commitment to Unity	"One God . . . who is over all" (4:6)
Eph. 4:7–13	Complement of Giftedness	"Attaining to . . . the fullness of Christ" (4:13)
Eph. 4:14–16	Concern for Body Growth	"Grow up into . . . Christ . . . and . . . in love" (4:15–16)

Together they constitute a blueprint for Christian ministry, each part vital to the makings of the whole. Thus we can say that the focus of Christian ministry is that *God's law of growth is unity, diversity, and bringing men to maturity in love.* In any study of Christian ministry and the church, these principles must be central theses and commitments of a local assembly.

The farmer reminds us of the importance of starting out carefully. If in a field or garden your first rows are not straight, that affects the layout of your entire farming enterprise. So it is with understanding Christian ministry in the church. The first rows are most important. If we can accurately establish what is the essential character of the church, we have uncovered the foundation for our study, which will lend itself to a stable and sound structure for building a biblical philosophy of ministry. The rows of the character and conduct of the church will produce a harvest of Christian ministry.

Yet competitors and counterfeits abound. Our modern ministry theory and practice offers many systems of evaluation that press against the character of the church. Initially we can say that any theory or view, any group or ministry emphasis, any denomination or parachurch concern, any method or practice that pulls at the fabric of the unity and oneness of the Body of Christ is suspect and to be weeded out. Regardless of past activities and traditions,

BIBLICAL PHILOSOPHY OF MINISTRY

Figure 1

institutionalized or not, our standard must always go back to those first rows that see every believer as "one in Christ Jesus," and each saint doing his part as the body "builds itself up in love!"

Now for the rest of the field!

4

Biblical Relationships: Crucial Building Blocks for the Church

In the midst of the barkers and booths along the ministry midway, confusion can abound about priorities for the church. Tired traditions, like bad habits, die hard. It takes mental discipline to get through these mazes. Remembering that our bearing is always in the Scripture ("Do not go beyond what is written," 1 Cor. 4:6b), we have attempted to establish the reality of who we are in Christ as a body of believers. Paul has exclaimed, "For you are all one in Christ Jesus" (Gal. 3:28d). The essence or character of the Body of Christ is unity—a oneness—a likeness of being that discards worldly distinctions. Based on that oneness, which is strategically rooted in the character of our God (Deut. 6:4; Eph. 4:4–6), we stretch ourselves out in ministry commitments. These commitments include prizing our diversities, or grace gifts in the body, and promoting individual maturity and corporate growth—in love.

BACK TO THE BASICS

How do you eat an elephant? One bite at a time. Such is the situation with Christian ministry in the church. First, we size up the project, *then* we break out the tableware. Checking our blueprint for ministry, we do well to look first at the Author of that blueprint and the guidelines He set down for accomplishing the task.

> Hearing that Jesus had silenced the Sadducees, the Pharisees got together. One of them, an expert in the law, tested him with this question: "Teacher, which is the greatest commandment in the Law?" Jesus replied: "Love the Lord your God with all your heart and with all your soul and with all your mind. This is the first and greatest commandment. And the second is like it: Love your neighbor as yourself. All the Law and the Prophets hang on these two commandments. (Matt. 22:34-40)

Talk about a crash course in Old Testament introduction! Jesus, having demonstrated before the Sadducees His ability to interpret with power and clarity the truths and acts of the Old Testament, was confronted by a master in legal and rabbinic interpretation. The Pharisee's inquiry was seemingly genuine and sincere, for Mark records that he approved of Jesus' reply and consequently was not far from the kingdom of God (Mark 12:32-34). Actually, Jewish theology was not entirely off target. It taught that God was entirely unique and without comparison (Mark 12:32; cf. Deut. 4:35; Deut. 6:4). Yet saying and believing, knowing and doing, were mutually exclusive for the tradition-bound Jew. It followed carefully from the uniqueness of the character of Yahweh that allegiance and affections must result. Saying leads to believing and to loving. In this the Jew was deficient.

LOVING THE LORD

Believers as lovers. Few concepts have greater implications. We are commanded to "love the Lord your God with all your heart, soul, and mind." Again this is agape love. It is a willful love, a determined love, a generous choosing of the interest of another over oneself. In this case it is loving the Lord—the Lord your God. Having seen the blueprint, we love the Author. Hearing the Word of God and receiving the Incarnate Word as Savior results in guided affections.

Note two important concerns. First, this is your Lord. Of the whats and hows, this is the what. He is Lord not merely known but personally embraced. This action cannot be accomplished as a static theological concept. The whole of the 613 Old Testament commandments is summarized in the preoccupation of a true worshiper of the one and only living God. Love is not a term of affection cast adrift in the sea of religious enthusiasm. It is rather lashed to the lover of the true God. It is intimately related to the Source of intimacy. These are scenes of endearment; they are glimpses beyond the courtyards of pretense and Pharisaism into the chambers of the devout. Nothing less is the message of the law and the prophets.

The second follows from the first. This love, or willful affection, is by means of every fiber of a believer's being. This is the how. Heart, soul, and mind. Affections, will, and intellect. This is integrated intimacy. It is a devout and true believer whose preoccupation with his Lord increases and constantly takes over new territory in his life. The Old Testament barometer for this whole-person commitment was obedience.

> And now, O Israel, what does the LORD your God ask of you but to fear the LORD your God, to walk in all his ways, to love him, to serve the LORD your God with all your heart and with all your soul, and to observe the LORD's commands and decrees that I am giving you today for your own good? (Deut. 10:12–13)

Fearing, walking, and serving are forms of obedience. No wonder this first and great command was planted in the context of obedience that resulted in prosperity and blessing from the Lord (Deut. 6:1–2).

To this point we have seen love as directional. It is a dimensional relationship with its first-dimension being the vertical focus of a believer toward his God and Lord in a wholehearted love and obedience.

LOVING OUR NEIGHBOR

But Lord, you don't know my neighbor! I mean we call our neighborhood "the valley of the shadow!" The local Little League team is nicknamed "The Piranhas!" They devour everything in their path between home and the ball diamond!

"And the second is like it: Love your neighbor as yourself." Many believers long for idyllic fields of ministry. If only most of their time could be spent in the books. They could emerge from their study just long enough to wax eloquent on the latest nuances of lapsarianism and synergism. Yet this example was never the teaching or the model of our Lord. He said the key teaching from the Old Testament commandments is that men are to be genuine lovers: lovers of God *and* lovers of men. In the trenches of a world system controlled by Satan, in the foxholes of homes that promote values contrary to Scripture, and in relationships with men and women blinded by sin, we are to live out our love for the Lord.

The legal expert who had posed the questions concerning the greatest commandment had a personal problem. We are not told exactly what it was, except that it concerned matters of "inheriting eternal life" and that he became increasingly convicted as Jesus spoke. Consequently, he tried to justify himself by retreating to the arena he knew best—the one of debate over definitions and theological precisions.

> But he wanted to justify himself, so he asked Jesus, "And who is my neighbor?" In reply Jesus said: "A man was going down from Jerusalem to Jericho, when he fell into the hands of robbers. They stripped him of his clothes, beat him and went away, leaving him half dead. A priest happened to be going down the same road, and when he saw the man, he passed by on the other side. So too, a Levite, when he came to the place and saw him, passed by on the other side. But a Samaritan, as he traveled, came where the man was; and when he saw him, he took pity on him. He went to him and bandaged his wounds, pouring on oil and wine. Then he put the man on his own donkey, took him to an inn and took care of him. The next day he took out two silver coins and gave them to the innkeeper. 'Look after him,' he said, 'and when I return, I will reimburse you for any extra expense you may have.' Which of these three do you think was a neighbor to the man who fell into the hands of robbers?" The expert in the law replied, "The one who had mercy on him." Jesus told him, "Go and do likewise." (Luke 10:29–37)

The legal expert must have squirmed inwardly during Jesus' telling of this story. Just as the priest and Levite had skillfully maneuvered past the beaten traveler, so he had dodged the basic issues of life and godliness of these great commands. Likewise, he had attempted to divert attention from the real issue at hand to matters of theological esoterism. But the story was clear. Clearly, the Samaritan, dread the thought, had been the true neighbor. Neighborliness had nothing to do with religious garments, titles, or blood lines. It was defined as "the one who had mercy on him."

If we are neighbors insomuch as we are givers of mercy, then our neighbor is one whose need we see and whose need we can meet. Willful or determined affection toward the Lord must issue in consistently similar behavior toward those around us. The Scriptures, and our Lord, have no commendations for those who restrict their worship of God to vertical and private matters of affection alone. There is a wonderful and privileged duty in learning of our Lord and taking that knowledge and gospel to those around us in contexts of friendship and expressions of mercy.

Now we see that love is multidimensional. The second dimension is the horizontal focus of a believer toward those around him—a commitment to loving others, being givers of mercy, and above all placing the interests and needs of others above ourselves (the model of *agape*).

Loving our neighbor as applied to other believers. Jesus gives careful guidelines for greatness—Christian ministry as it is applied to relationships within the body—to a group of followers who were competing to be the most favored.

> Then the mother of Zebedee's sons came to Jesus with her sons and, kneeling down, asked a favor of him. "What is it you want?" he asked. She said, "Grant that one of these two sons of mine may sit at your right and the other at your left in your kingdom." (Matt. 20:20–21)

Reasonable enough. Concern for status, for rank. The remarkable thing about this request is that the disciples had just received promises of great status and place in the kingdom as co-regents over the tribes of Israel (19:28). But, was that position worthy enough for one who had given up so much to follow the Messiah? Thus the not-private-enough private request.

> When the ten heard about this, they were indignant with the two brothers. Jesus called them together and said, "You know that the rulers of the Gentiles lord it over them, and their high officials exercise authority over them. Not so with you. Instead, whoever wants to become great among you must be your servant, and whoever wants to be first must be your slave—just as the Son of Man did not come to be served, but to serve, and to give his life as a ransom for many." (20:24–28)

Greatness and spiritual status, in Christ's eyes, are seen strictly in terms of servanthood and faithfulness (cf. 1 Cor. 3:5; 4:1–2). The dual concerns of model and motive are answered. Our model is "the Son of Man [who] did not come to be served, but to serve," and our motive is grounded in the atonement done on our behalf as He gave "his life as a ransom for many."

In our ministry midway, no prize attracts quite like the prize of success. This offer, beckoning to the believer from almost every booth, is held out as the ultimate in ministry rewards.

Ah, the sweet smell of success. Heads turn. People notice. Things happen. Success. Everyone knows what it is. It is achievement. It is what we wear, what we drive, the size of our group or building, the clout of our bank account, the career status we push to achieve. Whether the memo comes from the corporate headquarters of Amway, IBM, or Xerox, the message is the same: Believe in yourself, love yourself, and be successful. Ambition becomes the elixir that allows someone to get ahead—even if he has to step on a few other people. Ambition means literally "to canvas for promotion." This heady wine, promoted by our world system, has blurred our perspective on ministry and life, has distorted family units, and has blurred our understanding of the church.

When this message of success comes from corporate America, that is no surprise. The surprise comes when this same message begins to slip, with increasing persistence, into the words and counsel of believers and Christian leaders. Whatever may be the generally accepted business principles for our free-enterprise system, we must not transfer those same principles into the theology of Christian ministry. To the saint who has the bearing and courage to remember Christ's guidelines in Matthew 20, he finds standards based on real spiritual activity for measuring true success.

Loving our neighbor as applied to unbelievers. Remarkably, Christ did not distinguish neighbors on the basis of regenerated status. Simply, if in our passing by we see someone in distress or need and we have the opportunity and means to help, then that is enough. We are to give aid.

The Jews had an extensive legal code for distinguishing between the Gentile and Jew. All Gentile newborns were considered unclean. It was a violation of Jewish law to help the pagan Gentile in any way or to rescue a Gentile from danger. Jewish physicians were not to help Gentile women who were in personal danger in childbirth. Jews were not to associate with, or keep company with, Gentiles in any social setting. In short, there was bitter hatred between the Jew and Gentile.

Yet Christ cut across those barriers. In the story of the Good Samaritan, the mercy-giver was a Samaritan. The non-neighbors were the Jewish religious leaders. In all ways Christ was saying that giving aid as an expression of loving my neighbor as

BIBLICAL PHILOSOPHY OF MINISTRY

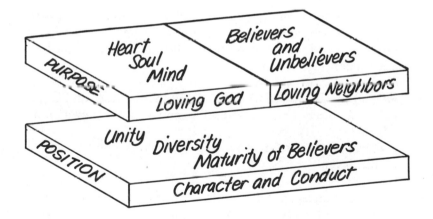

Figure 2

myself is based simply on need—considering each man as worthy and worth helping. No distinction is made based on race, gender, socio-economic status, or creed.

As if to reaffirm this emphasis, Paul continues these thoughts in his writings.

> Let us not become weary in doing good, for at the proper time we will reap a harvest if we do not give up. Therefore, as we have opportunity, let us do good to all people, especially to those who belong to the family of believers. (Gal. 6:9–10)

Extending ourselves to the needs of others, whether it is in the context of someone caught in a sin (6:1–2) or harvesting the results of patterned living (6:7–8), is consistent with the commands and teaching of our Lord. Anyone who makes a claim to be a lover of the Lord carries with him the responsibility for extending that same affection to those around him.

MULTIDIMENSIONAL RELATIONSHIPS IN THE CHURCH

The two-fold emphasis of our Lord in Matthew 22 and the corresponding responsibilities of believers to believers and believers to unbelievers leads us to a basic conclusion. There are three basic relational concerns for the church:

- First dimension—relationship between a believer and God
- Second dimension—relationship between a believer and a believer
- Third dimension—relationship between a believer and an unbeliever

The first dimension, representing "loving the Lord your God," is vertical and two-way. The second and third dimensions, representing "loving your neighbor as yourself" are horizontal and also two-way.

FIRST-DIMENSIONAL RELATIONSHIPS

The first-dimensional relationship is between a believer and God. It is established on the basis of Christ's work on the cross for us. Once a person trusts Christ as his Savior, the work of the cross is complete in redemption. The work of reconciliation is accomplished.

Yet that is only the beginning. For the Old Testament saint, the beginning was God's sovereign work in choosing Abraham, and through him making a nation that mirrored His character and work in the world. Yet a whole code of instruction, namely the law of Moses, was also laid out to give that saint the boundaries by which he could walk in obedience to God. That was, and is, fellowship with God. Fellowship is a mutual sharing between two parties (cf. 1 John 1:5–10). This progressive fellowship, or friendship, first between God and Abraham and then the children of Israel, reflected God's desire for a mutual and reciprocal relationship between Himself and those made "in His image and likeness." In Christ's words, that represents the believer who is drawing deeply and regularly on the truth of "loving the Lord your God with all your heart and soul and mind."

SECOND-DIMENSIONAL RELATIONSHIPS

The second-dimensional relationship is between a believer and another believer. Its basis is again the work of Christ. Two brothers are now members of the Body of Christ and equally heirs together of the grace of God. Hence, because of union in the Body of Christ, there is no qualitative distinction between them.

Since the church is made up of many individual believers, the corporate body of believers creates an even more involved interplay of multiple relationships. Christ's expectation was for His disciples to follow His model and preoccupy themselves with serving others rather than being served. That commitment to agape love within the Body of Christ creates fellowship between believers as well as fellowship between believers and God (1 John 1:1–4).

As the Body of Christ functions in genuine ministry, relationships grow and Christ's instructions concerning "loving your neighbor as yourself" are accomplished. Suffice it to say that without this fabric of interrelationships within the Body of Christ, the reverse effect begins to happen. The life usually expressed in a maturing local assembly becomes lifeless. This cannot help but have a negative impact on whatever relationships and contacts exist between believers and unbelievers in the third dimension.

THIRD-DIMENSIONAL RELATIONSHIPS

We know it is hard to accept, but believers are supposed to have relationships with unbelievers. That is the third-dimensional relationship of ministry. With-ness leads to witness.

God begins that reaching out by the convicting work of the Holy Spirit (John 16:8–11) as He draws men to Himself (cf. John 6:44). The God-ordained blend of divine work combined with relationships being developed by a believer toward his unbelieving neighbor results in the salvation of many.

It is not surprising, therefore, that Christ was concerned about both vertical and horizontal relationships in life. This became the fulfillment of the whole of the Old Testament and the summation of ministry as taught by the Lord Jesus Christ:

> A new commandment I give you: Love one another. As I have loved you, so you must love one another. All men will know that you are my disciples if you love one another. (John 13:34–35)

The ability of the disciples to love one another had a direct bearing on the ability of *all* men to identify them and their Lord.

FAILURE: THE SEEDPLOT FOR GROWING STRONG LOVERS (John 21:1-17)

Now the thought that may sneak into the back of your mind in the midst of this discussion is, *What if I fail?* These are lofty standards. I can see, from Ephesians 4:15–16 as well as from Matthew 22, the necessity of cultivating my life according to the standard of love; first, as a lover of my Lord, and second, as a lover of others—my neighbor included. But what if I can't measure up. How does the Lord look at my failure in this regard? Believers in the Body of Christ for generations have asked these very same questions and have fled quickly to the life and lessons of the apostle Peter. In John 21, Peter was at the low point of his life, not long after his denial of the Lord. He had been at the forefront as a spokesman for the twelve, proclaiming the truth of Jesus as Messiah. Now, having denied the Lord, Peter had gone back to what he knew best—fishing. The Lord met the eleven disciples on the shoreline and, after eventual recognition, began to talk to and eat with His friends. After what must have included some awkward silences in their meal together (21:12), Jesus turned to Peter and began to inquire about his affections toward Him.

> When they had finished eating, Jesus said to Simon Peter, "Simon son of John, do you truly love me more than these?" "Yes, Lord," he said, "you know that I love you." Jesus said, "Feed my lambs." Again

Jesus said, "Simon son of John, do you truly love me?" He answered, "Yes, Lord, you know that I love you." Jesus said, "Take care of my sheep." The third time he said to him, "Simon son of John, do you love me?" He said, "Lord, you know all things; you know that I love you." Jesus said, "Feed my sheep." (John 21:15–17)

This section of Scripture, in our judgment, is one of the sweetest and most tender. Jesus asked Peter three times, "Do you love me?" The essence of that Scripture is lost in the English. But before we explain the nuance of the original text, we must encourage you for a minute with your English text. The difference between understanding the biblical message in the original language and in a good English translation, of which there are a number today, is like the difference between watching a television program in black and white and watching one in color. You may get a richer, more precise glimpse of the picture on the color set, but both television sets will have accurately portrayed the basic message of the program. So it is with reading the New Testament. We can appreciate the additional glimpse the Greek gives us into the meaning, but we can be confident that we can know the message of the Bible in a good modern English translation.

The first time Christ asked, "Peter, do you *agapao* me?" Peter responded, "I *phileo* you." Christ was asking, "Peter, are you willing to 'generously choose My interests over your own'? Can you extend yourself beyond the natural, brotherly affections of *phileo* to the willful and determined affections of *agapao*?" All Peter could do is respond, "*Phileo*." This happened a first and a second time.

But in the third question, which understandably caused Peter distress because of his three denials, Christ came down to the level of *phileo*. He said, "Simon, son of John, do you love (*phileo*) me?" Peter is able to respond at the level of *phileo* and the injunction comes, "Shepherd my sheep."

Christ has pronounced a very careful principle concerning the progressive ability of believers in matters of becoming skillful lovers. The principle is this: Although God's standard for ministry affections is *agape*, He is infinitely compassionate with us at the level of our struggle and more than willing to meet us at that level as we continue to obey Him. Our struggles and failures form the backdrop for learning how to reach out in faith and love to our Lord and to others. It also says that we are to get on with the work of the ministry, whatever our level of maturity and ability.

One final question. Did Peter learn the lesson?

> Now that you have purified yourselves by obeying the truth so that you have sincere love for your brothers, love one another deeply, from the heart. (1 Pet. 1:22)

Again looking at this verse through the Greek we find different words for our English word *love*. Peter is saying the following: These believers have begun their spiritual pilgrimage by obedience to the truth that has purified them. Now, with a *phileo* love for the brothers, they are told to reach deeply and have *agape* love for one another from the heart. He did learn the lesson of John 21. He learned that it is a regular, normal experience of believers to mature in their abilities to love the Lord and one another.

Do not get devastated by your failures, or slowed down by your inabilities, or sidetracked by wanting to be the favorite. By the grace of God, keep moving. Keep making those conscious and willful decisions for agape.

CONCLUSIONS

Farmers understand the principal parts of farming: roots and fruit. Those two concerns, when added to proper soil preparation and planting, good irrigation and weather, and good care for the young plants from infancy to maturity will likely result in a good harvest.

We also have begun our spiritual farming project in this book. We have identified the need for starting right—getting our rows planted straight. If we understand who we are in Christ and what our basic ministry task is within the Body, we have started well. But we admitted the existence of weeds—competitors that challenge the reality of who we are in the Body.

Now the *roots* of our faith are in Christ, and as such they are defined in the words and concepts of life as He saw it. We discovered three major root structures designed to produce health in the Body of Christ. These structures are our relationship to God, our relationship to other believers, and our relationship to the world. God's concern is that our root system be strong and that we be growing and maturing in our abilities as lovers. He wants our affections to be monitored by the Scriptures in such a way that a fruitful harvest for the kingdom of God is assured.

5

Christ's Perspective on Christian Ministry

A diligent farmer is concerned about his crops' root systems the way a believer is concerned about the root systems of his ministry. Just as productive crops demand strong, healthy roots, even so growing and maturing believers are rooted in the soul of agape — branching off into a love for the Lord, a love for other believers, and a love for unbelievers, wherever needs are seen that can be met.

The Moore family is seeing these principles being worked out in exciting ways in their community. In addition to the joy of sharing their lives with the students and faculty-staff family at Multnomah School of the Bible, they are surrounded with ministry opportunities at home and in their semi-rural church body. Yet, beyond responsibilities to each other as a family unit at home, to the school, and to the local assembly, they are excited about their growing ministry with our neighbors.

They have lived at the present location in the wooded foothills of Mt. Hood near Portland since 1977. The Lord provided them with a home and some acreage to practice the family art of "gentleman farming." When they moved in, they began cultivating a friendship with their nearest neighbors. They are a family of eight — joined by assorted goats, horses, and barn critters. As a family, the Moores began to express their concern and love for their neighbors in the most creative and energetic ways they could imagine. They have prayed for them regularly. As needs developed, they were as available as time and skills allowed. The relationship with them, and love for them, has grown steadily during these years. Presently, though the parents have made no known commitment to Christ, the Moores can honestly say that they, as a family, genuinely love that family. They understand that the friendship with them is not conditional. They do not need to act a certain way, or speak a certain way, or believe the same way, in order to maintain a friendship. They consider this family our special friends and are trusting that they, as a family, will soon come to faith in Christ Jesus. "Loving my neighbor as myself" involves extending ourselves beyond our Christian comfort zones into lives and relationships that allow the "loving the Lord my God" to be demonstrated in practical ways.

We've given you this background on the ministry commitments of John's family on purpose. We think the ministry emphasis of Matthew 22:34–40 forms an important backdrop to the concerns and instructions of Christ to the eleven after His resurrection. This instruction is seen in Matthew 28:16–20 and is referred to as the Great Commission.

DISCIPLE-MAKING AND THE CHURCH

Public relations. Proclaiming the message through media. Worldwide enterprise. Sound familiar? Such is the stuff Christian method and ministry is made of today. Without making final judgment on the aforementioned emphases, it nevertheless is instructive to note that the initial patterns for ministry by the Lord were distinctively different from methods we might naturally think of.

> Then the eleven disciples went to Galilee, to the mountain where Jesus had told them to go. When they saw him, they worshiped him; but some doubted. Then Jesus came to them and said, "All authority in heaven and on earth has been given to me. Therefore go and make disciples of all nations, baptizing them in the name of the Father and of the Son and of the Holy Spirit, and teaching them to obey everything I have commanded you. And surely I will be with you always, to the very end of the age." (Matt. 28:16–20)

Some strategy! Christ was regathering the eleven. Just before that meeting the disciples were fearful and discouraged, confused and overwhelmed by the turn of events in Jerusalem. The prophecy of Zechariah concerning the striking of the shepherd and the scatter-

BIBLICAL PHILOSOPHY OF MINISTRY

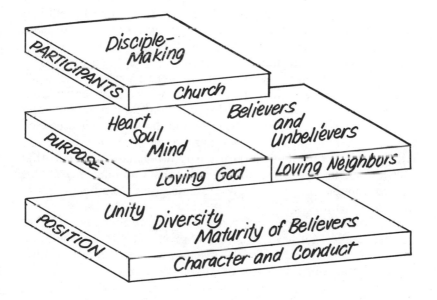

Figure 3

ing of the sheep had been fulfilled. Now in further fulfillment of the events following His resurrection, Christ was meeting His disciples in the familiar setting of Galilee (Matt. 26:32; cf. Zech. 13:7). That was where Christ and the disciples had begun almost four years earlier (Matt. 4:12–22). For nearly a year those men had stayed with Christ, learning of Him. The next two years were spent in the Galilean region, followed by their taking the gospel message into Judea and Perea in the last six months preceding the final week in Jerusalem. Now they were back home near an unnamed but evidently familiar mountain (28:16). With a mixture of joy and doubt (28:17; cf. 28:8) they greeted Jesus.

The risen (not yet ascended) Lord had accomplished His work of atonement on the cross. "All authority" in heaven and earth was His. The ministry mandate given in Matthew 28 has two pertinent backdrops from other passages in Matthew that apply to the church. First, in Matthew 16:13–20 heaven and earth had been a similar concern. With great prophetic power and precision Christ had affirmed the confession of Peter concerning His rightful claim as Messiah. Building on that, He predicted just that— a building program. But not with the modern connotation of brick and mortar; rather, Christ meant buildings of flesh and blood. There is a critical difference. Christ predicted that upon Peter and the other apostles He would build His church. Further, He predicted that there would be a divine-human cooperation in the project, whereby the authority and efforts would be shared. He saw that even the gates of hell would not prevent its advancement. This was the prediction of the New Testament church's beginning in universal form.

A second, less-known reference to the church adds a further perspective. In Matthew 18:17 Christ gives guidelines for admonishment in the Body of Christ—discipline of the sinning brother —within the four-fold steps of 18:15–17. These guidelines are reinforced with key epistolary references (cf. 1 Cor. 5:1–5; 9:11; 11:30; 2 Thess. 3:6–15; 1 Tim. 5:19–20). This was the preview of the existence and partial ministry of the local church meeting together to proclaim Christ, build up the local members, and take the gospel to others who have not heard.

Two references. One citing the majesty of the messianic promises, and the other focusing on the agony of how to deal with a sinning brother. One looking to the whole of the Body of Christ. The other looking to the local expression of the whole. Both form a vital part of the ministry task of the Great Commission.

DISCIPLE-MAKING: THE MANDATE

As we have seen in chapter 4, Christ had already given clear and forceful instruction on the essentials of ministry, based on the greatest commandments of the Old Testament. We are to be lovers of God and lovers of others. Matthew 28:19–20a is a further definition of how that is to be accomplished. Disciple-making is the key verb in this passage. It is the barometer that all ministry tasks are to be measured against in the church. Measurements in "nickels, numbers, and noise," or other sundry concerns ultimately must be held accountable to this passage. If our efforts are primarily to build into the lives of the saints, then we can be confident we are building on the right ministry foundation.

The ministry is more than many secondary matters associated with modern Christian endeavors—matters that look more at physical rather than human assets. All too often, unfortunately, it is the tail wagging the dog in Christendom. It is the budget, or the construction program, or the Christian school that determines ministry directions. Observe that Christ would have none of that. His concern was people—disciples—and all other competitors for top billing in the ministry were skillfully avoided.

Christ's preoccupation was with a ministry process that transferred truths from the teacher into the lives of the disciples (Luke 6:40). His focus was on quality, not quantity; multiplication, not addition. He selectively chose a few. He kept narrowing the audience of His message to those "who had ears to hear." He often drew Peter, James, and John away from even the twelve for private instruction. His concern was for building only one kingdom—the kingdom of His Father.

Disciples never prosper from production-line treatment. We sometimes look at the church as we would a large herd of steers. Each steer has our membership or denominational brand. But by face or name or individual, they are unknown. Yet we dutifully drive them to plush pastures, assuming all the while that they are developing personally as disciples. Then we wonder why the church is not functioning as a healthy body.

Once a week John meets with a group of men from different churches, sharing a common commitment to the Lord Jesus Christ. They eat breakfast together, study the Word together, and write out personal applications of the text, which then are shared for the purpose of prayer and personal follow-up, where appropriate. In ministry terms, that is a highlight to John's week. The regular inter-action of men who share a love for the Lord and for one other, and are able to make progress at both levels in the context of gentle accountability, is without equal for growing disciples. Actually, to women in the Body of Christ, this is no surprise. They have been doing it for years. But as men, we have not done well in matters of support and expressed affection. Yet the pattern of Christ's ministry and the instruction of the epistles (cf. Tit. 2:1–7) clearly speak to a people-priority above any competing voice.

The emphasis on disciple-making in the Great Commission has three qualifiers: going, baptizing, and teaching. *Going* expresses the overall pattern for disciple-making. We are to be a people who are regularly looking around in relation to the needs of others. This is the beginning of the extension of the "loving your neighbor as yourself" into unknown territory. In matters of Christian ministry, we have settled into the following: "Actually, I'm open to ministry—either at home or overseas. But I think it wise to stay put unless God clearly shows me I should go." We would submit that that thinking is backward. Rather, we should be saying, "I think it most consistent with the Scriptures that I go—unless God clearly shows me I should stay." Such an emphasis would fit well with the pattern of Christ and the twelve, who had an urgency for going that carried them into the needs and lives of those around them, and beyond (Matt. 9:13; 10:6–7; 18:12).

But *going* is only the general pattern as presented by Christ in Matthew. The definitive steps of discipleship are the next two: baptizing and teaching.

DISCIPLE-MAKING: THE DIVINE TWO-STEP

A disciple is a student, a learner. Everything about the term and the teaching of Christ shouts, "Process!" It is a process that begins with the hearing of the Word that results in conversion. This conversion places a believer into the Body of Christ (1 Cor. 12:12–13).

The discipleship process contains two major parts: baptizing and teaching. Baptism as a concept reminds us of John's baptism and the baptism of Christ (Matt. 3:1–17). John's baptism was a baptism of repentance. It was associated with the need for a changed life. For believers, it was associated with their sins (3:6). For the religious leaders, it focused on fruit (3:8, 10). It was turning away from an old pattern of life and thinking rightly and anew concerning the kingdom of God and the Messiah.

Christ's baptism was both the same as and different from John's baptism. It was the same in that it signaled something new. It was the initial presentation of Christ. It brought the proclamation of the Father concerning His Son: "This is my Son, whom I love; with him I am well pleased" (3:17). Yet it was immensely different. In the life of Christ there was no sin or hypocrisy. There needed to be no confession of and turning away from sin. For Christ, His baptism was a word of proclamation, of divine approval. Likewise, baptism for us "in the name of the Father, the Son, and the Holy Spirit" becomes a proclamation of divine approval.

Baptism and repentance. Baptism and obedience, for the production of fruit. For the disciple, baptism in a public forum becomes the first step in fruit production, the first step in considering seriously the cost of following Christ. Thus, we are not surprised when we read, "This is to my Father's glory, that you bear much fruit, showing yourselves to be my disciples" (John 15:8). From the beginning of Christ's ministry, baptism and discipleship have been intimately joined. Baptism, though being de-emphasized in modern ministry circles, remains the vital first way a child of the King understands that his conversion is to result in a changed life, inwardly and outwardly. It is the understanding of the possible "gains" and "losses" in the kingdom of God, while being kept securely in the eternal hands of the Father (John 15:1–8; cf. 10:27–30; 1 Cor. 3:15; 5:5).

Teaching ensures the finishing of the disciple making process. It is teaching others to live out the truths Christ espoused. Notice that He says, "Teaching them to obey everything I have commanded you" (Matt. 28:20a). It is Truth wedded to life. The standard for teaching is complete obedience—obedience in everything. The commission, or mandate, in Matthew 28 thus becomes a lifetime project.

Of course Christ personified the master teacher. From the masterful interpretations of the law to the instruction of His disciples He modeled the truth He taught (Matt. 5:1—7:28; 28:19–20). The term *teaching* appears strategically in Matthew's gospel. It depicts both the message and method of Christ's ministry in contrast to the presentation of the religious leaders.

Christ's message was clearly taught: "Jesus went throughout Galilee, teaching in their synagogues, preaching the good news of the kingdom" (Matt. 4:23a). It was the message of the kingdom—the good news that God had acted on behalf of and had sent the Messiah to secure redemption from sin. Even later the enemies of

Christ begrudgingly admitted that He taught "the way of God" (Matt. 22:16). It was a message of good news and hope, and it was a message given with authority (Matt. 7:29; 13:54; 21:23). Christ's method was to take the message regularly to the masses, particularly to places of religious inquiry (Matt. 9:35; 11:1; 13:54; 26:55).

But every good plan seems to encounter competing elements. There were competitors in Christ's day—men who equally taught about the ways of God—yet from a bias and twist that was exposed by Christ. The first hint of that is in Matthew 5:19. In speaking of the righteousness of the religious leaders, Christ warned against breaking any of the commandments and against teaching others to do so. In other words, the religious leaders were doing the very opposite of what they espoused. This is precisely brought out by Matthew later in his gospel:

> Thus you nullify the word of God for the sake of your tradition. You hypocrites! Isaiah was right when he prophesied about you: these people honor me with their lips, but their hearts are far from me. They worship me in vain; their teachings are but rules taught by men. (Matt. 15:6b–9)

Straight talk on a stiff subject. Christ pinpointed the patterns of the Pharisees and scribes. They had so twisted and interpreted the Old Testament laws that they had actually invalidated them. They were nullifying and breaking the greatest commandment, to "love the Lord your God with all your heart . . . soul [and] . . . mind." Thus, Isaiah's indictment became Christ's as well. That was powerful stuff for a proud people.

DISCIPLE-MAKING AND THE FINAL COMFORT

The disciples were about to embark on a mystery voyage. Their lives were soon to encounter what is one of the mysteries of Christ and His Body in our present age. Christ is both with us and absent from us as we wait for His return. Christ ended the Great Commission with words of comfort, "And surely I will be with you always, to the very end of the age" (Matt. 28:20b). Shortly Christ would rendezvous with His disciples again. That time in Jerusalem He would give them final instructions about the spread of the gospel and then be "taken up before their very eyes" (Acts 1:1–9). Worked carefully into the fabric of Christ's ministry that He was leaving His disciples were threads of comfort—His continuing presence with them. He would never leave them. Until the end of the age as they knew it, He would remain. This is true for us also. All of the effort and commitment and instruction and obedience is accompanied by the presence of Christ Himself. Not just a mystery—a final comfort!

CONCLUSIONS

Loving your Lord and loving your neighbor. This is the whole of the Christian message. Having begun the pilgrimage by hearing the gospel and receiving Christ as Savior, the pilgrim is to continue his journey by encountering and overcoming two basic hurdles.

The first is *baptism*. Initial commitment. The second is the reception of *teaching*, which leads to obedience. Consistency. The indoctrination of the disciple-making process thus has two steps, or hurdles. For the newborn New Testament church, those steps began on the day of Pentecost and continued daily from then on (Acts 2:41–47). For others, the start is much slower. But for all true believers the race is on. The track is before us. The pace is faithfulness. The goal is increasing fellowship with Christ Himself, accompanied by the valued commendation "Disciple."

6

Church Ministry
in the Epistles

Before we can feel we have done justice to the study of Christian ministry, we must continue with a careful sampling from the epistles. We will have given an overview to the question in a systematic fashion—avoiding the temptation of simply providing a random proof-text of our conclusions. We have selected Scripture from Luke's historical account (Acts), from the early writings of Paul (Galatians), and from his later writings (1 Corinthians).

MINISTRY GUIDELINES AFTER THE CROSS

Calvary. All that the Lord had spoken to His disciples seemed to fade in a fog of confusion and fear. His last words had been directions for disciples. But how could that *now* be? The Master Discipler was gone! The One who would give direction and perspective had ascended to the Father. The answer begins to come to us in the book of Acts. For now *disciple-maker*, as a verbal concept of action, fades. But *disciple*, as a noun of substance, begins to appear. Now the one-way, unilateral relationship of a discipler to a disciplee disappears. It is replaced by a mutual relationship between two disciples. It is bilateral—two-way. It becomes brothers sharing a common faith and Lord and involvement in the mutual task of ministry. Lest we become overly absorbed in the discipleship concept as the all-encompassing perspective on Christian ministry, Acts and the epistles balance us out. After the book of Acts, the term *disciple* never reappears in the Scriptures, though we find similar concepts reviewed in different terms.

ACTS: REDISCOVERING OUR ROOTS

Hold on a minute. Acts is a transitional book. It seems a bit dangerous to draw ministry principles from a book that is caught up in the "changing of the guard" from an Old Testament economy of law to a New Testament perspective of grace and truth in Christ (cf. John 1:17).

However, rather than seeing Acts as a transitional book it seems better to see it as a book of transitions. That is, it does record the inception of the New Testament church—the indwelling and abundant ministry of the Spirit of God to believers and the proclamation of the gospel to people who had not heard. But to admit this is hardly to admit a defect in the book. For we must remember that all Scripture is from God and is profitable for multiple ministries in the body (cf. 2 Tim. 3:10–17). We should be able to discern principles for church ministry in the book of Acts while also discerning important interpretive matters.

Acts 2:42–47. Just as we can tell much about a plant by the life of its roots, so we can tell much about the life of the church by studying its roots in Acts 2. Because of the message of Peter's sermon—a sermon motivated by Christ's final directions (Acts 1)—great conviction swept through the festival crowds at Jerusalem. Three thousand people experienced repentance, conversion, and baptism on that first day. The life of the plant had sprung up quickly; it could not be ignored. The reason for this is seen clearly in the verses following:

> They devoted themselves to the apostles' teaching and to the fellowship, to the breaking of bread and to prayer. Everyone was filled with awe, and many wonders and miraculous signs were done by the apostles. All the believers were together and had everything in common. Selling their possessions and goods, they gave to anyone as he had need. Every day they continued to meet together in the temple courts. They broke bread in their homes and ate together with glad and sincere hearts, praising God and enjoying the favor of all the people. And the Lord added to their number daily those who were being saved.

We find the root structure of the early church reflected in the multidimensional relationships observed from the gospel of Matthew. Once again they include the following:

- First dimension—relationship between a believer and God
- Second dimension—relationship between a believer and a believer
- Third dimension—relationship between a believer and an unbeliever

First-dimensional relationship. "They devoted themselves to the apostles' teaching" (Acts 2:42). As we have learned, Christ places the highest priority on a believer's walk with God. The greatest pursuit of man is to "love the Lord your God with all your heart . . . soul [and] . . . mind" (Matt. 22:37). The young church understood that there was no separation between loving the Lord and loving His Word, which was given by the Holy Spirit through the apostles (2 Pet. 1:20–21). Although it is a serious charge to label a brother a "bibliolater," we suspect the New Testament church, in the proper sense, came close to that. The members were resolute in their conviction that God's will was revealed in Scripture. They were devoted to the apostles' doctrine as a means of better knowing and loving their Lord.

Acts 2:42 shows that unity is never at a greater level than at the doctrinal level. Ephesians 4:13 instructs us that the church's goal is to be built up "until we all reach unity in the faith and in the knowledge of the Son of God and become mature." Of course, our love is beyond the printed page of doctrine to the Person of the Lord. Yet we hold up the written Scriptures as our guide for godly living (2 Pet. 1:1–11).

Second-dimensional relationship. Loving our Lord leads to loving our neighbor. The vertical leads to the horizontal. This love was expressed in the early church by continual devotion to fellowship, the breaking of bread, and prayer. Those three commitments complemented the devotion to the apostles' teaching, or the Scriptures. They give us a glimpse into the internal life of the church—the lifeblood of intimacy—that continually nurtured the young organism.

Fellowship is sharing—giving what you have to others who have need. It is from the root *koinos*, which carries the idea of having things in common: both tangible, in terms of property and possessions, and intangible, in terms of relationships and attitudes. In this passage, in a strong spirit of Christian community, Luke tells us that these believers "had everything in common." They either shared their physical goods or converted their possessions to cash for the purpose of giving to anyone who had need. There is a difference, however, between Christian community and communal activity. In the American communes of the 1960s, young people, including believers, sometimes shared too much. There were times that the clear guidelines for life-style and moral conduct were violated. The Scriptures are clear on two points: first, commitment to fellowship in the early church was not mandated— it was voluntary; and second, it was in the context of other equally clear standards for marital and individual behavior. Christian community (which we believe will develop in America as we realize the implications of these and other New Testament texts), cannot function properly without the input of mature Christian leaders in local church contexts, and it cannot prosper under decree or legislation. It must be rooted in the conviction of the individual believer's conscience. From Acts 4:32–35 we see that the apostles directed and donated funds and that "there were no needy persons among them" (Acts 4:34*a*).

But, you say, that was the early church. Certainly God cannot expect similar behavior, albeit voluntary, in the church today. Let us see what Paul says:

> Our desire is not that others might be relieved while you are hard pressed, but that there might be equality. At the present time your plenty will supply what they need, so that in turn their plenty will supply what you need. Then there will be equality, as it is written: "He that gathered much did not have too much, and he that gathered little did not have too little." (2 Cor. 8:13–15)

Surprised? The goal is the same as that worked out historically in the early church. The principle is equality: no believer is to have too much, and no believer is to have too little. This commitment to voluntarily giving to meet the needs of others in the Body of Christ is a continuing desire of God. A final caution: "Each man should give what he has decided in his heart to give, not reluctantly or under compulsion, for God loves a cheerful giver" (2 Cor. 9:7).

These truths were dramatically impressed on the Moore family a few years ago. They decided to sell their home and some acreage and build a smaller home on adjoining property. They were going to build this new home on the equity left over from the selling of the first home. Their motivation was essentially to free their family from a mortgage obligation and make do with a smaller home. But, to allow even an interim arrangement on the undeveloped property next door, they had to drill a well so that, at relatively short notice, they could vacate their present home as they prepared to build their new, smaller, home. To their surprise, the new well went 375 feet, but they had enough money to go only 200 feet. They were beginning a theological education that they had not planned.

A few days later John was having lunch with a Christian friend who, after a good and extended conversation about many things, asked him how the well project was going. Upon explaining the situation to him, he committed to, and later wrote a check for, the considerable balance still owed on the well. He gave the Moore family the money on two conditions: first, the money was a gift, not a loan; second, they were to continue to understand their biblical obligation, albeit voluntary, to minister to the needs of others out of their "plenty." That strongly encouraged their development of applying the principle of equality as God gives opportunity.

But this text in Acts 2 also instructs us in matters of worship. The early church was committed to the breaking of bread (public worship) and prayer (both public and private worship). The Lord's Table seemed to be the central focus of the church meeting. We learn from 1 Corinthians 11 that the assembly regularly examined themselves (in relation to sin) and proclaimed the Lord's Person and work, looking to His imminent return (cf. 1 Cor. 11:23–28). It continued throughout the life and growth of the church: believers gathered on the first day of the week "to break bread" (Acts 20:7*a*).

Prayer was also vital to these young believers; substantial time and priority was given to it. Believers joined their hearts and minds together in intercession for the needs of those around them—for the dangers and problems facing the church (cf. Acts 4:23–31; 6:4–6; 12:12–17). The needs of the church regularly brought these believers to their knees in intercession to their Lord.

Third-dimensional relationship. "Praising God and enjoying the favor of all the people" (Acts 2:47). In the Scriptures the gaining of salvation and inheritance in the kingdom of God is never the final goal of the Christian life. The church was also gripped with a mandate to *go* to the unsaved around them.

Evangelism as a life-style was a vital feature of the New Testament church. This text ends with reminding us that these believers were "praising God and enjoying the favor of all the people. And the Lord added to their number daily those who were being saved" (2:47). That is the final part of ministry. It is *favor evangelism:* commitment to relationships with unbelievers, which, in the context of friendships, leads to new birth. This new birth, given by God, was accomplished in the midst of favor and affection between believers and nonbelievers. The precedent for this is seen in the life of Christ Himself, at the young age of twelve, and the principle is continued in the writings of the apostle Peter (cf. Luke 2:52; 1 Pet. 3:15).

Priorities and pressure (Acts 6:1–7).

> In those days when the number of disciples was increasing, the Grecian Jews among them complained against those of the Aramaic-speaking community because their widows were being overlooked in the daily distribution of food. So the Twelve gathered all the disciples together and said, "It would not be right for us to neglect the ministry of the word of God in order to wait on tables. Brothers, choose seven men from among you who are known to be full of the Spirit and wisdom. We will turn this responsibility over to them and will give our attention to prayer and the ministry of the word."
>
> This proposal pleased the whole group. They chose Stephen, a man full of faith and of the Holy Spirit; also Philip, Procorus, Nicanor, Timos, Parmenas, and Nicolas from Antioch, a convert to Judaism. They presented these men to the apostles, who prayed and laid their hands on them.
>
> So the word of God spread. The number of disciples in Jerusalem increased rapidly, and a large number of priests became obedient to the faith.

There is no gain without pain. Genuine intimacy always develops in the midst of adversity. Not only is this true in an individual believer's walk with his Lord, but also with the gathered assembly.

The book of Acts records some major growing pains of the early church. In Acts 5, the Lord took the lives of Ananias and Sapphira before the evil caused by their lies and deceptions spread throughout the church. And the church learned the lesson (5:11). In Acts 6, new problems developed. Some of the believers, of Greek origin, believed their widows' basic needs were being neglected. The church had to confront a paramount problem: maintaining the principle of equality of goods in the face of potential divisiveness based on culture and background.

The solution was found in the cooperation of the twelve with the disciples. The apostles understood their responsibilities as primarily directing the church at Jerusalem through prayer and the ministering of the Word. The serving of the widows, though no less a ministry, needed to be delegated to men of proved leadership and spirituality in the assembly. The seven were selected by the congregation of disciples, and, after being set apart by the apostles, began to meet the needs of the widows. It is observed that the spreading of the Word of God and the influence and ministry of the church was strategically linked to the same priorities seen in Acts 2. Loving the Lord and His Word and loving others, both in the Body of Christ and outside of it, remained the mainstay for the life of the church.

Spiritual and Numerical Growth (Acts 9:31).

> Then the church throughout Judea, Galilee and Samaria enjoyed a time of peace. It was strengthened; and encouraged by the Holy Spirit, it grew in numbers, living in the fear of the Lord.

After the dramatic conversion and early ministry of Saul of Tarsus, the church in Palestine grew at an increasing rate. Saul added a new and dynamic addition to the church that was not without its demand on the body of believers (cf. Acts 9:19b–31). Yet in Acts 9:31 we see a continuation of the same emphases that the Lord began in the church in Acts 2.

First, the body's relationship with the Lord grew. The Holy Spirit gave strength and encouragement to the assembly. The fear of the Lord brought wisdom and growth. Second, relationships in the body developed. There was a strong sense of cooperation in the assembly in protecting Saul from the Jews' plots to kill Him. And third, increased outreach to the unsaved was reflected in the church's growth.

This should always be the order. Sinking our roots deep into the soil of our love for our Lord, we branch out in love to believers around us. And that most important spiritual growth results in the gospel's going to those who do not know Christ. Spiritual growth then produces numerical growth.

GALATIANS: GUIDELINES FOR GROWTH

One of Paul's earliest epistles, evidently written before the Jerusalem Council of A.D. 50, is the epistle to the Galatians. The issue was critical: these believers wanted to add to the gospel message. Paul decided to confront this challenge to the faith head-on.

Pursuing conduct consistent with the gospel (Gal. 1:6–10).

> I am astonished that you are so quickly deserting the one who called you by the grace of Christ and are turning to a different gospel—which is really no gospel at all. Evidently some people are throwing you into confusion and are trying to pervert the gospel of Christ. But even if we or an angel from heaven should preach a gospel other than the one we preached to you, let him be eternally condemned! As we have already said, so now I say again: If anybody is preaching to you a gospel other than what you accepted, let him be eternally condemned!
>
> Am I now trying to win the approval of men, or of God? Or am I trying to please men? If I were still trying to please men, I would not be a servant of Christ.

Paul quickly pulls out the stops in this epistle. There was a different gospel—literally, a non-gospel—being preached. The fallacy was on two levels: first, a different content; and second, a different commendation.

The different content was the addition of the demands of the law to the grace and righteousness of Christ.

> We who are Jews by birth and not "Gentile sinners" know that a man is not justified by observing the law, but by faith in Jesus Christ. So we, too, have put our faith in Christ Jesus that we may be justified by faith in Christ and not be observing the law, because by observing the law no one will be justified.
>
> If, while we seek to be justified in Christ, it becomes evident that we ourselves are sinners, does that mean that Christ promotes sin? Absolutely not! . . . I have been crucified with Christ and I no longer live, but Christ lives in me. The life I live in the body, I live by faith in the Son of God who loved me and gave himself for me. I do not set aside the grace of God, for if righteousness could be gained through the law, Christ died for nothing! (Gal. 2:15–17, 20–21)

Recognizing that no man can fully comply with the righteous demands of the law, Paul reaffirms the true gospel, which is salvation by faith in Christ Jesus. The false gospel, that is, adding to the work of Christ merits of the law, was perversion and confusion and deserved the fullest condemnation of God (Gal.

BIBLICAL PHILOSOPHY OF MINISTRY

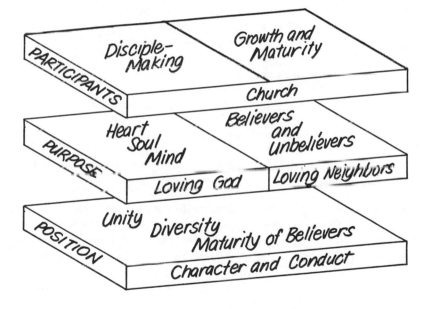

Figure 4

1:7, 9). The implications were clear: "If righteousness could be gained through the law, Christ died for nothing!" (Gal. 2:21).

This false gospel also offered a different commendation. Paul recognizes the potential danger in trying to please men rather than God (Gal. 1:10). Just as a slave cannot serve two masters, so Paul cannot be a servant to both man and God. Since this gospel came from God and not man (Gal. 1:11), Paul affirms the necessity of serving God by proclaiming the true gospel.

One reason this issue was important to Paul is seen in the life of Peter. This apostle spent years struggling with the issue of partiality toward Jewish brethren. Peter's desire to gain the approval of men, that is, James and the Jewish converts, caused him to favor association with the Jews. Paul does not spare words in confronting his fellow apostle. He states that Peter was not "acting in line with the truth of the gospel" (Gal. 2:14). Any conduct that disregards the vital facts of the gospel is implicit denial of the truth of the gospel. But, was Peter the only one with a problem?

Spiritual living—by the Spirit (Gal. 3:1–3).

> You foolish Galatians! Who has bewitched you? Before your very eyes Jesus Christ was clearly portrayed as crucified. I would like to learn just one thing from you: Did you receive the Spirit by observing the law, or by believing what you heard? Are you so foolish? After beginning with the Spirit, are you now trying to attain your goal by human effort?

Consistency! The "Peter Principle" was also the Galatian Principle. These believers were forgetting they were in Christ. Their life in Christ had begun by the Spirit and needed to continue by the Spirit. No contribution of the flesh could cooperate with the Spirit to bring about spiritual maturity.

Paul develops this truth, and the implications of it, in terms of warfare:

> So I say, live by the Spirit, and you will not gratify the desires of the sinful nature. For the sinful nature desires what is contrary to the Spirit, and the Spirit what is contrary to the sinful nature. They are in conflict with each other, so that you do not do what you want. But if you are led by the Spirit, you are not under the law. (Gal. 5:16–18)

Believers are engaged in war. There is a constant battle between the flesh and the Spirit in all believers. In other words, the flesh is always only too willing to cooperate with false doctrine or wayward commendations to confuse the believer. But the intent of the Spirit of God is for a walk that is consistent with the Person of Christ Himself (cf. Gal. 5:22–25). Confusion at the foundation weakens the whole structure. An important part of Christian ministry is understanding the sound doctrines of the gospel of Christ, which will produce a life of godliness.

Spiritual ministry—by the Spirit (Gal. 6:7–10). Having planted the good seed of the gospel of Christ, Paul now speaks about the harvest:

> Do not be deceived: God cannot be mocked. A man reaps what he sows. The one who sows to please his sinful nature, from that nature will reap destruction; the one who sows to please the Spirit, from the Spirit will reap eternal life. Let us not become weary in doing good, for at the proper time we will reap a harvest if we do not give up. Therefore, as we have opportunity, let us do good to all people, especially to those who belong to the family of believers.

This arena for warfare is also analogous to a farmer's field. The habitual ways of thinking and acting produce a harvest. If our habits by the flesh result in sin, then we harvest destruction (cf. Gal. 5:26—6:1). The believer's growth is stopped based on poor decisions as a spiritual farmer. If our activities involve "doing good to all people," then our harvest is plentiful and results in a well-run race (cf. Gal. 6:2–5; 1 Cor. 9:24–27; 1 Pet. 3:3–9). Notice the twofold emphasis. We are to carry concerns for *all* those around us; believers and nonbelievers alike.

1 CORINTHIANS: CORRECTING CHURCH CONDUCT

As was mentioned earlier in chapter 2, the church at Corinth was full of both problems and possibilities. They were a knowledgeable church—yet proud. They were a gifted assembly—yet divided.

Co-laborers with the eternal God (1 Cor. 1:10–12).

> I appeal to you, brothers, in the name of our Lord Jesus Christ, that all of you agree with one another so that there may be no divisions among you and that you may be perfectly united in mind and thought. My brothers, some from Chloe's household have informed me that

there are quarrels among you. What I mean is this: One of you says, "I follow Paul"; another, "I follow Apollos"; another, "I follow Cephas"; still another, "I follow Christ."

Paul knew a storm was about to hit Corinth. Based on both known information and reports from other believers, he warns this church. There were quarrels (1 Cor. 1:11) that would lead soon to divisions (1 Cor. 1:10). Paul pleads with these believers to reconsider what they say about each other ("that all of you agree with one another") and what they think about each other ("that you may be perfectly united in mind and thought"). Verbal and mental unity were vital for church unity.

But his concerns for Corinth came from the implications of the preferences of these believers for the ministries of one over another.

> What, after all, is Apollos? And what is Paul? Only servants, through whom you came to believe—as the Lord has assigned to each his task. I planted the seed, Apollos watered it, but God made it grow. So neither he who plants nor he who waters is anything, but only God, who makes things grow. The man who plants and the man who waters have one purpose, and each will be rewarded according to his own labor. For we are God's fellow workers; you are God's field, God's building.
>
> By the grace God has given me, I laid a foundation as an expert builder, and someone else is building on it. But each one should be careful how he builds. For no one can lay any foundation other than the one already laid, which is Jesus Christ. If any man builds on this foundation using gold, silver, costly stones, wood, hay or straw, his work will be shown for what it is, because the Day will bring it to light. It will be revealed with fire, and the fire will test the quality of each man's work. If what he has built survives, he will receive his reward. If it is burned up, he will suffer loss; he himself will be saved, but only as one escaping through the flames. (1 Cor. 3:5–15)

This grouping of believers, based on the preference of style or emphases of doctrine of some men over others, was inconsistent with the whole sense of Christian ministry and growth in the church.

Remembering the lessons of Matthew 20, Paul emphasizes the measure for a believer's success: servanthood. Apollos, Peter, and Paul were to be regarded only as faithful servants (1 Cor. 4:1–2). The Corinthians were acting as though the work of the ministry rested on men rather than God. For purposes of emphasis, Paul says this twice (1 Cor. 3:7–8). That is joined to the other emphasis of the paragraph: men are co-laborers with God in spiritual farming. God has ordered His sovereign purposes for His church according to the means of human cooperation. That does not change the fact God is the ultimate source for growth. But, servants can plant and water in cooperative fashion with God Himself!

This, then, is a single purpose in ministry and allows *no* place for division. The single purpose for men in the ministry, that is, cooperation with God in the harvest, binds us together. Apollos, Peter, and Paul can be appreciated for unique contributions to the church, but that is no excuse for separating contributions and valuing some men over others.

Paul made a unique contribution: he laid the foundation. Yet the builder is not to be remembered—the foundation is. The foundation is Jesus Christ. Paul reminds these believers that preferential treatment of some over others was a distraction away from the Head of the church. Man's work is to be judged according to its ability to proclaim Jesus Christ. If one seeks self-exaltation then he is in danger of judgment (cf. 4:3–5). Ministries promoted out of false motives will disappear and have no lasting value or reward. But ministries rooted in the foundation of Christ will endure. These sobering words should cause us to constantly reevaluate our ministry efforts according to these terms.

Do you feel the pressure from the expectations of our day? Conversations between believers concerning the health of respective assemblies quickly move to matters of "nickels, noise, and numbers." At pastoral conventions the almost-exclusive measure of success is in numerical terms. But, God's concern is for the cultivation of faithful servants able to appreciate diverse ministries without entertaining divisiveness.

People have asked Ken, "How is your church going?" He answers the question strictly in terms of perceived spiritual growth in the body and in his own life, and in the impact in the community. He often notices a nervous twitch in his inquirer. "Well, that's wonderful, Ken. But, what I mean is, how is the church *really* doing?" Trying to avoid the obvious, Ken repeats his former answer and adds observations about specific issues of spiritual growth. But that does not satisfy his friend. Finally, with some exasperation, he says, "Actually, Ken, what I mean is, how large is your church? How many members are attending? What are the building plans?" Ken had been talking about a building program, but the questions were obviously coming from a different level.

It is time for candor in the Christian church. We are not going to see the Body of Christ prosper if it follows the path of traditional expectations and conventional credentials. Spiritual health is seen in spreading the Word of God and developing disciples. Numerical growth can no more be the standard for success in the church than the book of Acts can be our textbook for Christian ministry to the exclusion of the epistles and the rest of Scripture. God is concerned about developing body growers, not body counters! Remember the caution: "His work will be shown for what it is, because the Day will bring it to light" (1 Cor. 3:13a).

REPRODUCING MATURITY:
AVOIDING THE SPIRITUAL GENERATION GAP

It is easy to forget, but worth remembering: few things are forever! Fads and fashions, notions and nations, passions and possessions. All are going back to dust. But the kingdom of God is eternal. God, His Word, and His children. We can find no other things more worthy of our time and effort.

The Spirit of God has reserved for us, in the last writing from the hand of Paul, a record of ministry priorities that answer the question of how to reproduce spirituality and Christian maturity.

> You then, my son, be strong in the grace that is in Christ Jesus. And the things you have heard me say in the presence of many witnesses entrust to reliable men who will also be qualified to teach others. (2 Tim. 2:1–2)

The biblical starting point is very familiar to us. All Christian ministry begins with God Himself. We are to draw deeply on the grace of Christ as an expression of "loving the Lord": being before doing. If Timothy, as he ministers to the church of Ephesus, can strengthen himself at this level, he can handle every pressure the ministry can offer, focusing on reproducing maturity in the lives in the assembly.

Just as love for the Lord produces love for your neighbor, spiritual growth produces spiritual investments in the lives of those around you. This is the disciple-making pattern working out in the life of the maturing church. In this passage four generations are in view: the first two are past; the last two picture the future health of the church.

The first generation, for Timothy's concern, is Paul himself. To Timothy, Paul had been like a father (1 Cor. 4:17; Phil. 2:19–22). Paul's commitment as a spiritual father model led to Timothy's strong growth in the faith. Everybody needs a role model, a spiritual parent, who can inspire and encourage spiritual growth. For Timothy, it was Paul. For Paul, it was Barnabas. Growth cannot come in the body without the ministry and models of spiritual leaders.

The second generation is the "many witnesses." Paul did not act alone, or minister alone. That would have been inconsistent with his understanding of the church as a body and would have been counterproductive to the ministry principles we have seen so far. There were others—witnesses. They were confirmers of the faith, co-laborers with Paul. In Paul's last written "breath" in 2 Timothy 4:19–21, he mentions at least nine fellow witnesses.

The third generation is "reliable," or faithful, men. Just as a soldier or an athlete is in training, so a saint (cf. 2 Tim. 2:3–5). His training involves concern for the spiritual condition of himself and of those around him. Those around him are to take this faithful one aside and begin to teach him the truths of the grace of Jesus Christ. There is testing before serving and proving before pressure (cf. 1 Tim. 3:10). We are to prepare the young for the long race.

The fourth generation is the final stages of a ministry of multiplication. It is men who are not only faithful but who also share their knowledge and experience. In Christian ministry, the credentials are not principally academic, but experiential. In the New Testament, teaching is both content and context, orthodoxy and orthopraxy. Nothing less earns the ministry title in the Body of Christ of "qualified teacher."

CONCLUSIONS

Recently John had the privilege of teaching in 1 Corinthians 6 in their local assembly. He could not avoid 6:13*a:* "Food for the stomach and the stomach for food—but God will destroy them both." His children have gleefully seized upon this principle! Every time he tries to reason with them about how, since daddies have bigger bodies, they should have bigger desserts, they protest on theological grounds.

So it is in the Body of Christ. We have all kinds of teachers offering guidelines for ministry—beckoning for attention—promoting a shape for the body that is entirely unhealthy. We need more ministers like John's children, who caution the body at the most basic level and remind us of nutritious spiritual principles.

Loving the Lord and loving our neighbor. Devotion to the Scriptures and to the Body of Christ. Worship that is proper in public and genuine in private. The gospel reaching out to those who have not heard.

That's good food . . . for the Body!

Section 3

Biblical Aspects of Church Ministry, or The Main Thing Is that the Main Thing Always Remains the Main Thing

7

Organization and Meetings of the Church

In the film *Camelot*, the good King Arthur faced many dilemmas in the rule of his kingdom. But he had a secret weapon. When, in a battle scene, he wanted to survey the whole of the battlefield, he would, by the magic of Merlin, be turned into an owl, who could then soar over field and forest. This would give Arthur a view of the whole problem at hand, from which he could make wise decisions for his kingdom.

We have been attempting the same. Before we became lost in the trees of exegesis and prooftexting on matters of the church and Christian ministry, we surveyed the forest. From the patterns of the lives of Jesus and His disciples to the principles recorded in Acts and the epistles we have looked at the large picture.

We are now ready to examine a few very significant trees. In this section we want to look at some fundamental aspects of the New Testament ministry, including the form of the church and the function of its leadership and body parts.

ORGANIZATION OF THE CHURCH

Ideally there ought to be only one Christian Church throughout the whole world, the Church of Christ, one in doctrine, one in worship, one in government, one in discipline. Romanists and Episcopalians have no monopoly of the formula "one holy catholic, and apostolic

- church." Division within the church arose from unfaithfulness to Christ and declension from the apostolic pattern. Everyone imbued with zeal for the honour of Christ must deplore the fragmentation which has marred the body of Christ and to a large extent dissipated its witness.[1]

God has given function and honor to each member of the body "so that there should be no division in the body, but that its parts should have equal concern for each other" (1 Cor. 12:25). The precedent and concern for this is forcefully presented in the prayer of our Lord:

> My prayer is not for them alone. I pray also for those who will believe in me through their message, that all of them may be one, Father, just as you are in me and I am in you. May they also be in us so that the world may believe that you have sent me. (John 17:20–21)

As we have seen earlier, our unity in the body is grounded in the unity of the Godhead. The ability of believers to abide in this truth has a direct bearing on the message the world understands about the gospel of Christ.

The church is you who pray, not where you pray. It is an assembly of true believers. It is a gathering of Christians who have, as a common confession, the justification that comes by faith in Christ. The church is not where we go to worship; it is we who worship. It is not a building of brick and mortar. It is saints who, "like living stones, are being built into a spiritual house to be a holy priesthood, offering spiritual sacrifices acceptable to God through Jesus Christ" (1 Pet. 2:5). The only true church building is a living building of flesh and blood, the Body of Christ.

In recognizing these facts, the New Testament identifies three historic expressions of the church: the universal church, the city church, and the house church.

THE UNIVERSAL CHURCH

> And I tell you that you are Peter, and on this rock I will build my church, and the gates of Hades will not overcome it. (Matt. 16:18)

Inscribed in huge Roman letters from the Vulgate around the interior of the dome of Saint Peter's Cathedral in Rome are the

---

1. John Murray, *The Collected Writings of John Murray: The Claims of Truth, Vol. I.* (Carlisle, Pa.: Banner of Truth, 1978), p. 275.

BIBLICAL PHILOSOPHY OF MINISTRY

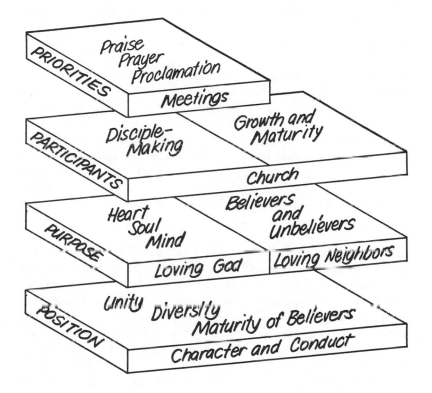

Figure 5

words of Matthew 16:18. Yet, as is seen above from the words of John Murray, no papal system or ecclesiastical institution has prior claim on what is the prediction and promise of the coming church.

The universal church is the Body of Christ and is bound together by the grace of the Lord Jesus. It is one even as Christ and the Father are one. There is no distinction or favoritism or special status given to some over others. Our foundation is Christ, and we are all "living stones, being built up into a spiritual house." In any community there is to be an affinity or recognition of a common brotherhood which goes beyond local church affiliation.

THE CITY CHURCH

This is the often-overlooked, more silent partner of the New Testament church. The Scriptures identify major population areas. The two most visible churches in the book of Acts are the church at Jerusalem and the church at Antioch.

Jerusalem was the focal hub of the early church. From there, and based on the instructions of Acts 1:8, the gospel began to spread through increasingly larger Jewish regions of the Roman Empire. The leadership of the Jerusalem church, the apostles, were responsible for the proclamation of the gospel and oversight of the newly-born flock.

The church at Antioch would become for the Gentile churches what Jerusalem was to the Jewish churches. The ministries and leadership of Barnabas and Saul were seen here, and from that city and surrounding churches relief for the Jerusalem saints was sent back to Jerusalem for the famine conditions that occurred during the reign of Claudius.

Although the churches of Jerusalem and Antioch were revealed in the New Testament writings as also meeting in house churches, it is instructive to observe that there was a city-identity to the church in those areas. The church reached out beyond the local houses and assemblies.

THE HOUSE CHURCH

The house churches of the New Testament formed the individual cells that made up the Body of Christ. Various house churches are acknowledged in the New Testament. A flock met in the home of Titius Justus (Acts 18:7); another met in the home of Aquila and Priscilla (Rom. 16:5; 1 Cor. 16:19). There were also assemblies that met in Nympha's and Philemon's homes (Col. 4:15; Philem. 2). Keeping in mind that the church is people and not a building, these homes served as buildings that housed the assembly during their meetings on the first day of the week, as well as during other occasions of worship, ministry, and prayer. As the believers in one area grew in numbers, they began to associate in a centralized location. This is seen at Corinth where they were coming together, from their homes, for a meal and the Lord's Table (1 Cor. 11:17–22). Thus, these house churches developed into local assemblies that met in public facilities.

Two important passages illustrate the relationship between different church types in the book of Acts. In Acts 2:42–47 we see the newly converted believers meeting together "in the temple courts" and breaking bread "in their homes" (Acts 2:46). There is, in that reference, a preview of the enthusiastic and joyful expressions of worship and fellowship that many New Testament communities would soon enjoy. The meetings in the Temple courts enabled this large and growing church to gather for times of corporate celebration. It revisited the place of the miracle of Pentecost and the exposition of the Scriptures by Peter concerning the Christ who was delivered up to the cross not only by them but ultimately by God on their behalf (Acts 2:22–24, 36).

The meetings in the homes were the local and geographic expressions of the effects of these believers' conversions being worked out in the neighborhoods of family and friends. Not only did they fellowship and share meals but, distinguished from their eating together, they "broke bread in their homes" (Acts 2:46). Following the instructions of the Lord, they were remembering Him through the Table—accompanied by the worship and praise of a church meeting.

The second passage that illustrates the interrelationships between the city and house churches is Acts 15. Here two city churches are in view: the church in Jerusalem and the church of Antioch. The problem was a severe threat—similar to the one addressed in the epistle to Galatia—and endangered the heart of the message of the gospel: "Unless you are circumcised according to the custom taught by Moses, you cannot be saved" (Acts 15:1).

Again false teachers were trying to add to the work of Christ by insisting upon the requirements of the law, namely circumcision, for the Gentile believers in Antioch. The danger was recognized by both Paul and Barnabas and the church in Antioch, and the two apostles were sent as a ministry team to Jerusalem to reach a consensus on the matter. The church of Antioch (Acts 15:3) is seen cooperating with the church of Jerusalem (Acts 15:4) in this important matter. Later, in reciprocal fashion, the church of Jerusalem sent the ministry team of Barsabbas and Silas to Antioch, along with Paul and Barnabas, to deliver the judgments of the council (Acts 15:22). There was a strong sense of cooperation in the ministry by these two city churches.

The message was sent "to the Gentile believers in Antioch, Syria and Cilicia" (Acts 15:23). Later, Paul and Silas, with the commendation of other believers, took the findings of the council "through Syria and Cilicia, strengthening the churches" (Acts 15:40–41). This, then, pictures the cooperative efforts of churches, both identified by city locations and beyond (possibly to house churches), as believers joined together in ministry and worship (cf. Acts 5:42).

So, when did we begin seeing churches as buildings rather than people? One of the most remarkable departures was the exodus of house groups as a unit of Christianity. The first recorded evidence of adopting a church building is between A.D. 240 and 245. In Dura Europos, a Roman garrison city on the Euphrates, archaeologists have discovered evidence of a house renovated for this purpose.

The owner moved out, and a dividing wall was demolished, allowing space for sixty to seventy participants. Benches were built in the courtyard. In a smaller room the congregants even built a baptistry with biblical motifs painted on the walls. Porphry, a pagan critic of Christianity during this time, records some painfully insightful observations: "But even the Christians mimic temple architecture and build vast buildings in which they come together to pray, which they could indeed do unhindered in their houses, since it is very well known that the Lord hears from everywhere."

Nothing is intrinsically wrong with buildings or the programs that go on in them. But we must remember that we do not need a major orientation to physical plants to accomplish spiritual goals. Our American communities look to buildings as credentials for a ministry effort; our Lord does not.

BODY MINISTRIES: INDEPENDENT OR INTERDEPENDENT?

The only problem with the above conclusions is that to the majority of believers today they would sound like conclusions found on the *Twilight Zone!* To actually consider that there is to be an enthusiastic and open willingness for cooperation and ministry between local assemblies and believers from different cities and geographic locations is foreign to most modern efforts of Christian ministry. We act more like marbles than grapes. When squeezed together we produce glass shards rather than sweet wine.

If we resist a spirit of cooperation and interdependence within the Body of Christ, then we are denying the reality of the Body of Christ. If we are single-minded in intent that all ministry meetings, efforts, and resources are to be used exclusively for one local church, or at least to point believers toward membership and participation in only one church, then we are denying the reality of the Body of Christ. If we do not join hands in our communities in matters of doctrine and discipline of believers, and cooperate energetically toward that end, then we are denying the reality of the Body of Christ.

Our failure to think clearly and act maturely has created a universal phenomenon in the Western church. We are divided according to social, economic, or racial lines, with gender gaps sprinkled liberally throughout. Such homogeneity should not exist in local churches. Entertaining these distinctions is like promoting theological racism. We forget that in the first-century church members of Caesar's house worshiped beside bondslaves; slave and slaveowner called each other "brother"; the Jerusalem church cared for Greek widows.

A local church should not be known for economic, professional, or racial distinctions. To examine another brother and think, *Well, yes, we are one in Christ, and yes, we are neighbors, but you really need to worship with your own kind*, is nothing less than partiality. It denies our very unity in Christ. Far too many believers think they can embrace God's kingdom yet practice partiality; regeneration in Christ makes little difference in their lives. It is time for Christians to abolish that sin.

Historically, the orthodox and fundamental churches in America have their roots in the struggles and schisms associated with the fundamentalist-liberal debates of the late nineteenth and early twentieth centuries. Our spiritual forefathers were fighters, and they needed to be. From their efforts, in major part, we have preserved the orthodox and biblical precedents that contribute to the strength of our assemblies today.

But it is also time to stop shooting our wounded. There is an identity and affiliation of believers in Christ that reaches beyond the memberships of local assemblies. In the New Testament, believers from house churches who lived in different cities cooperated in the ministry as a body. A hungry high schooler understands body cooperation—the stomach sends the signal to the brain, the eyes spot the targeted fast-food restaurant, the feet move, and the hands stuff the hamburger into the mouth. Believers, being convinced of the need for the cooperation of the foot, the eye, and the hand, must also join in the labor of the ministry. Our roots may have developed in the soil of independence, but our growth must come through a recognition of the cooperative efforts of assemblies and believers.

NEW TESTAMENT CHURCH MEETING

Any survey of the New Testament church meeting must first take into account the roots of the Old Testament, the nurturings of the gospels, the growth to maturity in the epistles, and finally the historic consideration of the church after the first century.

JEWISH ROOTS FOR THE NEW TESTAMENT MEETING—
BEFORE THE DEATH OF CHRIST

The roots of faith and the backdrop for the development of the New Testament meeting are found in the Old Testament itself. In some senses, the beginning of the scriptural account in the Garden looks at God's desire to meet with Adam and Eve. Because of the breach of fellowship caused by the sin of our first parents, and in its spread throughout the early peoples of the world, there developed within the plan of God the design and ministry of the Tabernacle.

From Moses to David the Jews met in the Tabernacle, or tent of meeting. This became the place for the offering of sacrifices for sins, for worship together during Israel's festival days, and the physical residence for occasional glimpses of the glory of the Lord. It was during this time, in Exodus 12, that Israel was commanded to institute the permanent memorial of the Passover and the Feast of Unleavened Bread. This not only reminded Israel of the deliverance of the nation but also prefigured Christ, who would be the final sacrifice and Passover (cf. 1 Cor. 5:7–8). These activities carried over similarly to the Temple from Solomon's reign until the dispersion of 586 B.C.

If the activities of Jewish believers at the Tabernacle and Temple form one major contribution to understanding the New Testament meeting, the existence of and activities surrounding the synagogue form the other. The synagogue, probably beginning during the captivity and further developed during the rule of the Greeks, was the standard expression of religious activity during New Testament times. The worship patterns, the officers, and the precedent of the synagogue left their mark from Matthew through Revelation.

There were three main elements to the synagogue service: praise, prayer, and proclamation of the Word of God. Praise in the Old Testament Psalms included both rejoicing in Yahweh for who He was (descriptive psalms) and reclaiming His faithfulness to Israel in the past (declarative psalms). This was done with joy and great congregational involvement. Synagogue prayers were recited from memory. They may have included portions of Old Testament passages or credal affirmations of the Jewish faith. And, of course, the declaring of the Word of God was a central part of these meetings. The message was often given by any man who could deal with the text adequately and was not limited to select rabbis of that given synagogue. It was within this context that Christ spoke to those in Nazareth from Isaiah 61:1-2 concerning the prediction and fulfillment of the blessings of the Lord (Luke 4:16-21).

The institution of the Lord's Table, or Supper, in the gospel also would become central to the later outworking of the New Testament meeting. As was said earlier, the festivals of Passover and Unleavened Bread form the backdrop for this ordinance, and Christ's instructions were clear. First, the bread, representing His body, was to be taken and eaten. Second, the cup as given represented His blood, which was shed for many. Third, Christ vowed not to drink again of the cup, after the final Passover, until "I can drink it anew with you in my Father's kingdom" (Matt. 26:26-30; Mark 14:22-26). This Table is later referred to in the book of Acts as the "breaking of bread."

HERITAGE OF THE NEW TESTAMENT MEETING—AFTER THE CROSS

It seems that, with good justification, any study on the church finds itself regularly back in Acts 2. Here we see the institution of the meeting of the church after the death of Christ and the events of Pentecost. Just as praise, prayer, and proclamation of the Word were characteristic of the synagogue service, so public praise, prayer, and the Word, as given in the doctrine of the apostles, were central to the early church. The first church meeting was to join in one heart and prayer to the Lord as they encountered the resistant religious leaders (Acts 4:23–31). Later church meetings in the book of Acts handled the matters of fair distribution to the widows (Acts 6), the imprisonment of Peter (Acts 12), the doctrinal challenges of the false teachers (Acts 15), and the instructions and final guidelines from Paul (Acts 20:7–12, 17–38).

In the epistles, Paul expands on the principles laid down in Acts. Matters of doctrine and discipline—praise and prayer—are seen regularly in his writing. In addition, guidelines are given for the selection of leadership for the churches and the ministries of gifted men and women in the assembly (chaps. 8–9).

The heritage of the regular gathering was established (cf. Heb. 3:13; 10:24–25). The New Testament meeting was to offer congregational praise and worship to the Lord. It consisted of the teaching of the Word, prayer, and elements of fellowship. The Lord's Table was regularly observed. The believers, meeting as the family of God in different geographic locations, exalted Christ. With teaching and admonishment, they functioned as a Body for the building up of the saints in love (Eph. 4:12–16; Col. 1:28).

HISTORY OF THE CHURCH MEETING—AFTER THE FIRST CENTURY

The study of the history of the church from the beginning of the second century yields a mixed bag. On the one hand, there remained the clear strains of doctrine and practice instituted in the Scriptures by Christ and the apostles. Yet, there also was developing some tendencies that were to have a detrimental effect on the church meeting.

On the positive side, the meetings continued on the first day of the week. There are indications the time was early in the morning (Pliny, A.D. 111–112). This followed the pattern of the New Testament and was in remembrance of the Lord's resurrection on the first day (Ignatius, A.D. 100–105). There were regular references to the Table of the Lord (*The Didache*, A.D. 100–130), the inclusion of the ordinance of baptism, and the regular care for the needy (Justin Martyr, *First Apology*, A.D. 151).

But where there is doctrine, there is also decay. Where there is liberty, there is also license or legalism. The history of the second century also brought into the church inclusions that were beyond the teachings of Scripture. Pliny cites the need for verbal oaths to the Lord; Ignatius begins a one-man crusade for the single head pastor, called the bishop; and Martyr suggests an atoning element to baptism.

Thus, the study of the church brings both confirmation and caution. It confirms what we have already seen, that is, the New Testament church meeting is a gathering of the saints for the purposes of teaching and fellowship. But it also cautions us not to exceed the Scriptures in matters of doctrine and life.

THE MEETING: BUILDING UP ONE CHURCH, OR ONE ANOTHER

In our day the church meeting has taken on some distinctive characteristics. We stand at the end of centuries of traditions, reactions, and overreactions to problems that have faced the church. Yet there are some emphases we should avoid.

First, the church is people, not programs. The Body of Christ is an organism that is designed to grow and develop as people minister to people. This is a difficult thing to program. The lifeblood of the body is relationships. If programs facilitate relationships, then they are justified. All too often, the opposite is true. The New Testament church meeting was orderly though unstructured; it encouraged involvement in the body, rather than the performance of the few (1 Cor. 14:26–33a). If the meeting agenda is largely restrictive and does not allow the regular inter-action of the body in terms of fellowship, prayer, and the Table, as well as the Scriptures, then the church meeting is going in the wrong direction.

Second, the church is participation, not professionalism. The body is to minister to the body. Members are not to be entertained. If the church specializes in hiring the best preacher, the best music director, and so on, then the body will never develop. Each part of the body is to say to the next: "I need you. I can't just hire someone to replace you. You are a valued part of this body." Nothing matures during dormancy.

Third, the church is to proclaim Christ, not promote itself. Try an experiment. Ask a close friend, "What is your church known for?" You will get a variety of responses. "Well, we have the finest pastor in our area! You should hear our choir. We have a staff of professionals and an expanding missions program. And finally, we have a fine church building, though we will have to start a new building program for our Christian school!" I think we have begun to turn the corner in Christian ministry when that saint says, "Our regular desire is to proclaim Him!" That cannot happen unless the doctrines of the church, as set forth in the Scriptures, become primary guidelines for the church.

There is to be a careful awareness among believers in our day of the realities of both the local assemblies and the Body of Christ. It is worthy and good to pursue ministry diligently in the fellowship of believers that is your church. It is detrimental to look at all Christian ministry and effort through this church lens alone. In the New Testament the Body of Christ met in separate congregations, yet at times joined together in matters that directly threatened the gospel message. We should do no less.

CONCLUSIONS

As Arthur the owl, we have had our flyover. We have also begun to look at some strategic trees in this ministry forest. But there are still some gaps left to be filled. These questions remain: How does the church view its leadership? How does the church view itself? How does the church view its families and the educational process?

These trees make up the next three chapters. And if we do our jobs well, then we are ready for the last, important question: Where do we go from here?

8

Leadership in the Church

Everyone looks for leadership models. It is part of the way God has made us—it is the nature of the learning process. John's learning from leaders has gone through three stages that might sound familiar to you.

Stage One. As a boy he grew up in strong denominational churches with strong single head pastors who directed the affairs of the church in strong and sometimes loud manners. Although he still appreciates much of what he learned in those childhood experiences, he concluded that pastors are the single and final authority on matters of God and man.

In his younger adult life this image was reinforced in strong nondenominational Bible churches. Again the strong and dynamic single head pastor did most of the preaching, directed the focus of the church, and functioned principally as "president of the corporation." He did find himself wondering where the headship of Christ would fit in this structure, but then he would put his head between his knees until the feeling passed! To his understanding, that was church leadership.

Stage Two. In both his seminary experiences, as well as in his pastoral responsibilities in the first two churches he served with, leadership was said to be multiple in form, commonly called a "plurality of elders." He did notice that more men seemed to be more involved in leadership, and he was thankful for that. But it still seemed that one man served as the focal point, the "senior pastor," the final answer on matters of faith and practice in the church. John did most of the teaching, as in the churches in stage one, and had special ministry responsibilities that were distinct from the lay leaders in the church. For all practical concerns, there were two types of elders modeled for him (and by him!) in stage two as well as stage one.

Stage Three. Eventually he found himself serving on a pastoral team with other elders who represented both secular and sacred vocational pursuits. They began to reevaluate the New Testament passages on leadership and came to some surprising, and for John, painful conclusions. It became harder and harder to make qualitative distinctions between clergy and laymen (staff and non-staff) elders. They could not find two types of New Testament elders. This pastoral team worked with him patiently for over a year as the traditional leadership models and areas of personal pride in his life began to be peeled off. They began to examine what the Scripture says about leadership and how indeed Christ is *the* Head of His church.

Leadership models? Few questions grip the church with quite the same fervor or frequency. Many of us have grown up under the nurture of godly church leaders and have at times assumed that what we have seen *is* the biblical model for leadership. But before we pour concrete over our conclusions, we need to evaluate our ideas in relation to the Scripture.

What is a leader? There is no agreement—at the definitional level:

- The ability of one person to influence or direct others (J. Oswald Sanders).
- The ability to rally men and women to a common purpose. It is a man who knows the road, who can keep ahead, and who can pull others after him (Field-Marshal Bernard Montgomery).
- It is the ability to get others to do what they don't want to do, and like it (President Harry Truman).
- There are three types of people: First, those that are movable; second, those that are immovable; and third, those that move them (Li Hung Chang).

In the world of imagery, we could have described a dynamic despot, a superhuman salesman, or a stirring strategist. Is the church leader a self-convinced, multi-gifted, corporate president?

BIBLICAL PHILOSOPHY OF MINISTRY

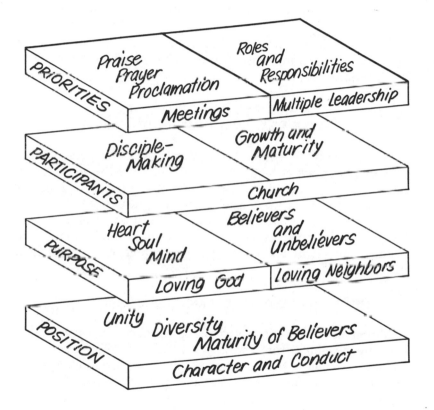

Figure 6

Is our mode for the church—not to mention the many parachurch organizations—the American corporation? Where does ambition fit, or does it? A. W. Tozer offers some alternative considerations:

> A true and safe leader is one who has no desire to lead, but is forced into a position of leadership by the Holy Spirit and external situations. A reliable rule of thumb is as follows: A man who is ambitious to lead is disqualified as a leader. A true leader will have no desire to lord it over God's heritage. He is rather ready to follow as well as lead.[1]

Is this description closer to the biblical model? Is there a place for a young man or woman *desiring* church leadership? A survey of pertinent biblical passages will help us with these questions.

BIBLICAL PRINCIPLES OF MALE LEADERSHIP AND MINISTRY

In any study of church leadership in the Scriptures, three principle tasks are at hand. First, there is a need to identify the biblical backdrop to the question—from the framework of the Old Testament and the gospels. Second, there needs to be an assessment of central passages in the New Testament as applicable to the church. Finally, there needs to be some understanding in distinguishing male and female leadership and responsibilities in the church.

LEADERSHIP IN THE OLD TESTAMENT AND THE GOSPELS

Abundant evidence in matters of spiritual conduct and leadership are available from the pages of the Old Testament. The history of Israel is the heritage of God-ordained leaders—men and women who found their adequacy in God. The model of the theocracy provided for a man to stand as the leader for the nation. Under the instructions of Yahweh, the ministries of Abraham, Isaac, Jacob, Moses, Joshua, and others provided a man, chosen by God, to be the go-between between God and the nation. Later, under the combined leadership of Saul, David, and Solomon, the rule of a king in Israel was instituted. Though the weaknesses of these men also affected the nation, they were used in significant ways in Israel. Therefore, the precedent of a single

1. A. W. Tozer, *The Reaper* (February 1962), p. 459.

leader (usually seen in the king motif) is clearly established in the Old Testament. Does this precedent become the proof for the authority and posture of the modern-day pastor?

In the gospels we begin to see a "changing of the guard." Jesus, who was and is "God with us," Immanuel, established Himself as heir to the claims and promises of Messiah and Lord. Later, as Peter proclaimed, "Therefore let all Israel be assured of this: God has made this Jesus, whom you crucified, both Lord and Christ" (Acts 2:36). For Jesus, in His Person and ultimately in His work on the cross, became *the* Mediator (1 Tim. 2:5-6).

The essentials of leadership in the gospels can be reduced to one passage: Matthew 20. Although numerous passages speak of the priorities and patterns of discipleship, leadership is defined in the gospels strictly in terms of *servanthood*. Greatness. First place. Top rank in the kingdom. Christ speaks to all those issues, and concludes: " . . . just as the Son of Man did not come to be served, but to serve, and to give his life as a ransom for many" (20:28).

Here, as developed in chapter four, is the *model and motive* for leadership. The model is the Son of Man—Jesus Himself. All that is known of greatness, of success, of first place in the kingdom is seen in Him. It is seen in His serving rather than being served. Jesus, for whom all things were created and by whom all things are sustained, left the majesty of the heavens and equality with God the Father, determined to serve and die for those dead in their trespasses and sin (Eph. 2:1-5; Phil. 2:5-8; Col. 1:15-17)! That is mercy.

If Jesus is the model for servanthood, the motive is self-sacrifice. Just as Jesus was the ransom for us, even so we are to give our lives for the flock of God. Peter speaks to this in his instructions to church leaders scattered throughout the Roman provinces:

> So then, those who suffer according to God's will should commit themselves to their faithful Creator and continue to do good.
> To the elders among you, I appeal as a fellow elder, a witness of Christ's sufferings and one who also will share in the glory to be revealed. (1 Pet. 4:19-5:1)

Ministry, suffering, and glory are seen as companion principles. Elders in the churches are to continue to do good, along with all the believers—understanding the relationship between suffering and sacrifice, and the glory and reward of serving the chief Shepherd (cf. 1 Pet. 4:1; 5:4). This becomes the leadership seedplot for growing ministry principles for church leaders in the epistles.

LEADERSHIP PRINCIPLES IN THE NEW TESTAMENT

In the epistles the activities and responsibilities of church leaders come to full blossom. Seven central passages contribute to the picture. From this, we should be ready to develop biblical principles for male leadership in the church.

In the New Testament three terms are used interchangeably to describe church leadership. They are *pastor-teachers, elders, and bishops.* The term pastor-teacher, taken from Ephesians 4:11, is one who shepherds. The pastor is guardian of the flock. Likewise, bishops were overseers for the church. Both terms look at the function of the church leader. The term elder speaks to the office, or position, of church leader. Although these terms may have slightly different emphases, they all speak of men who are given the ultimate human responsibility for the care of the church.

Leadership Respect and Service. Church life—cafeteria-style! So is the description of some concerning the selection of and commitment to a local assembly. The New Testament cautions against too casual an assessment of a believer's relationship to his church. Rather, there is to be careful appreciation and respect— recognizing the value of the contribution of other lives to ours and a recognition that there is *mutual accountability* as believers voluntarily submit to those over them.

1 Thessalonians 5:12-13

> Now we ask you, brothers, to respect those who work hard among you, who are over you in the Lord and who admonish you. Hold them in the highest regard in love because of their work.

If there were any illusions about the demand of the ministry on leaders in the church, that passage lays such thoughts to rest. At Thessalonica, the church had experienced the ministries of Paul, Silas, and Timothy. Now others were over them "in the Lord." Among the general admonishments for encouraging one another and building up one another (1 Thess. 5:11), the believers were reminded that they were to appreciate the labor of their leadership. Again, leaders are spoken of in the plural in the church of Thessalonica.

Hebrews 13:7, 17

> Remember your leaders, who spoke the work of God to you. Consider the outcome of their way of life and imitate their faith. . . . Obey your leaders and submit to their authority. They keep watch over you as men who must give an account. Obey them so that their work will be a joy, not a burden, for that would be of no advantage to you."

A number of rich truths concerning the life of the Body of Christ are given not only in these verses, but also throughout the chapter. These believers, struggling under the confusion of the relationship of the Old Testament to the faith (Heb. 2:1—3:18) and under the crucible of suffering and public humiliation (Heb. 10:32–39), are reminded of those that serve them in leadership in their assemblies. Though remaining unnamed, these leaders evidently lived exemplary lives. The writer of this epistle can confidently remind these believers of the leadership models they have, and encourage obedience for the advantage of the whole assembly.

Again, as in the Thessalonian passage, leadership is plural. There is no singling out of one as more significant than the others. The leaders both taught and lived the truths associated with the gospel of Jesus Christ. These believers were to aid in the ministry by cooperating with those over them. By now, the New Testament precedent was clearly set. God had reestablished a plurality of elders in each assembly for the purpose of shepherding the flock.

One final note. One case against plurality of elders among some is the affirmation that each believer is now a priest to God—that our need is now no human mediator—and that our access is to God in Christ directly. This is true and is repeatedly taught in Hebrews. But it should be noted that in this epistle that affirms the believer-priest status so clearly, we also find some of the strongest references to the leadership of elders in an assembly and the accountability of the individual believers to the leaders even as the leaders are accountable to God. The teaching of the believer's direct access to God in no way conflicts with the teaching of plurality of elders in the church.

Leadership responsibilities and shepherding. Recently John gained another new appreciation for a shepherd. At 1:00 A.M. he and his wife were launched out of bed by the hunting call of coyotes just beyond the pasture where the sheep were sleeping. Within two minutes John was with them in the pasture, talking to and comforting them, and leading them into the safety of the barn.

Settling back into the sack thirty minutes later, John was again impressed with the function of a shepherd. He is the one who stands between his sheep and danger. He is the one willing to take on the predator for the sake of his sheep. He is the one who has built trust among his flock so that, when danger comes, they follow him to safety. Talk about a crash course in practical theology! John should have had his pastoral students out in that field with him.

A pastoral ministry is very similar. Yet shepherding extends beyond the physical needs of the sheep to emotional and spiritual needs as well. The New Testament is fond of drawing on this agricultural model.

Acts 20:28

> Guard yourselves and all the flock of which the Holy Spirit has made you overseers. Be shepherds of the church of God, which he bought with his own blood.

This passage is a strategic Scripture for teaching a number of things about the church. The principal work of the leader is to guard and to shepherd. These functions both protect and provide for the sheep. The leader is the overseer who understands the joy of spiritual nurture and encouragement. Further, the clear message of this text is that the church is a work of God, for God, and by God.

The church is a work of God. The elders of the church at Ephesus are here called overseers. They are designated as officers of the church by the Holy Spirit Himself. The historic precedent for this is the church at Antioch, where the Holy Spirit through the church said, "Set apart for me Barnabas and Saul for the work to which I have called them" (Acts 13:2). The agency for appointment to church office is two-fold: the Holy Spirit and a spiritual assembly.

The church is a work for God. The work of the overseers is shepherding. Yet the work of human husbandry is toward the church, which belongs to God. The church's Head is Christ. The source of its leadership is the Holy Spirit. Thus, leaders are never laboring in *their* churches. They are shepherding the believers who make up the church that belongs to God.

Third, the church is a work by God. The last phrase of the verse reminds us that Christ, being God, has bought or redeemed the church by His blood. The work of Christ on the cross has bound Him and His body together for eternity. Any labor among church leadership is done recognizing that the ministry is accomplished on sanctified turf—it is with a body of believers whose identity is "in Christ."

The clear emphases of Acts 20 show who is the Pastor of the church! A few years ago a leading Christian journal interviewed two Christian authors on the subject of the church. The first author, well-known, likened the church to an orchestra. At first it was a volunteer effort—largely informal and without much organization —which slowly over the months becomes better known, larger, and in need of the organizational and leadership skills of a conductor. This picture, to him, illustrated the church, which is God's, and the need for a singular man to lead the group.

The second author responded with remarkable insight: "Well, yes, that is a beautiful illustration of the growth and cooperation of the church. The only difference is that you and I would disagree on who was the conductor."

All too often we miss the perspective of the divine because of our focus on the human. Indeed, God uses human shepherds to serve the flock of God. But we cannot lose sight of the fact that it is His church, not a man's; He is the Chief Shepherd, not a man; and that with Him as Master Conductor, the church has not a human but a divine Head.

Notice again that in both Acts 20:17 and Acts 20:28, we find elders or overseers (plural) with the church (singular). For the twentieth-century church, which is used to its billing and preoccupation centering on the single head pastor, he is yet to be found in our study. Actually, we shall discover in the New Testament passages that the single head pastor is conspicuous only by his absence.

1 Peter 5:1–5

To the elders among you, I appeal as a fellow elder, a witness of Christ's sufferings and one who also will share in the glory to be revealed: Be shepherds of God's flock that is under your care, serving as overseers—not because you must, but because you are willing, as God wants you to be; not greedy for money, but eager to serve; not lording it over those entrusted to you, but being examples to the flock.

And when the Chief Shepherd appears, you will receive the crown of glory that will never fade away.

Young men, in the same way be submissive to those who are older. Clothe yourselves with humility toward one another, because, "God opposes the proud but gives grace to the humble."

This remarkable passage further confirms our initial conclusions about leadership in the church. Note first the relationship between Peter and these elders. His words, his appeal, is as a fellow elder. Peter has learned the lesson of Matthew 20. No more maneuvering for position. No more preoccupation with comparisons. Now he refers to himself simply as a co-laborer—an equal. His expectation for these leaders is the same (1 Pet. 5:5).

As in the case of Paul's appeal to the Ephesian elders, here Peter challenges these leaders with the agricultural imagery of the sheep farmer. They are to care for their flocks even as a shepherd cares for his sheep. With an obvious parallel to Acts 20:28, Peter reminds these men that the believers in their churches are "under their care." They are cooperative caretakers of the flock of God. As such, they have three principal standards for conduct.

First, they are to serve out of personal motivation, not from obligation. They shepherd the flock because that is what they want rather than what they must do. Have you ever observed a parent caring for his child out of obligation? It is painful for the observer and for the child. That attitude pours acid on relationships. Leaders in the church dare not serve on that basis.

Second, they are to serve with enthusiasm. But here enthusiasm can be at one of two levels. A leader can be enthusiastic for the ministry, or he can be enthusiastic for the money. This is a caution repeated elsewhere (cf. 1 Tim. 6:10; Heb. 13:5). In areas of service to a church, a leader needs to be careful that his decisions and ministries are not motivated by personal gain.

Third, and most appropriately, leaders are to serve as examples, not as lords. In wording taken directly from the Gentile-style leadership mentioned in Matthew 20, Peter reminds these elders that you lead by following. The picture is of leaders who take advantage of their position. They lord it over those entrusted, or given, to them. They influence by position. Peter warns that leaders in the flock of God are models, not manipulators. Rewards from God are given in relation to the servant style of leadership (5:4).

As Peter writes this letter to be circulated and read in the churches, his instructions in this text speak to "elders [plural] among you." The exclusive illustrations of leadership in the New Testament assemblies are according to the model of multiple leadership.

Leadership roles among the saints. One of the old features of the twentieth-century church is what might be called the Little Jack Horner syndrome. Just as the poetic Jack, in the midst of breakfast, discovered his identity and significance with the plum, so church leaders today, particularly the younger variety, are encouraged to come to Jack Horner conclusions concerning their worth and ability in the ministry. The New Testament is much more cautious and encourages a consensus relationship that, in the least, looks to a local church for confirmation and direction for the ministry. Whether the leadership issue was service, or staff-relationships, the roles were defined within the context of the life and needs of the church.

Acts 14:23

> Paul and Barnabas appointed elders for them in each church and, with prayer and fasting, committed them to the Lord in whom they had put their trust.

As the gospel spread from its hub in Jerusalem to the Jewish and Gentile communities, Paul and Barnabas, from the church in Antioch, began to plant churches. These churches matured to the point where elders could be appointed. Being in familiar territory and with believers who had previously come to the Lord under their ministries, Paul and Barnabas appointed men to leadership positions. This is the first occurrence of elders in the New Testament church outside of Judea.

Notice carefully that elders (plural) were appointed in each church (singular). The beginnings of the principle of plurality of elders is seen in this passage. Each local assembly had a multiple of elders. Certain converts in these assemblies had matured as disciples of the Lord and, being given final instructions by Paul and Barnabas, were then appointed as elders in the church (cf. Acts 14:21–23). Evidently a church body can exist before elders are appointed. But elder appointment, when qualified men develop in the assembly, is an important feature of the maturing church.

James 5:14

> Is any one of you sick? He should call the elders of the church to pray over him and anoint him with oil in the name of the Lord.

In one of the earliest New Testament epistles, James writes to believers scattered among the Roman Empire. His instructions include spiritual remedies for spiritual/physical problems. The dilemma here could be exclusively physical or, from the preceding and following contexts, could include complication caused by sin. Regardless, the sick or weak one is to call for the elders so that prayers can be offered (and, presumably, confession, if applicable) for the recovery of the saint. Notice that again we see elders (plural) for the church (singular). Evidently plurality of elders, in each assembly, was a leadership principle begun early in the history of the New Testament church, and was broadly observed throughout the Empire.

1 Timothy 5:17

> The elders who direct the affairs of the church well are worthy of double honor, especially those whose work is preaching and teaching.

To many churches today, plurality of elders is a fine concept as long as a distinction of leadership is retained: (1) a *lay* class of elders who usually administer the programs of the church; and (2) a *professional* staff of elders, compensated as the paid staff of the church, who shepherd the spiritual affairs of the church. First Timothy 5:17 is often given as the prooftext for this view. While the text does make distinctions among elders, these differences are of degree, not kind. That is, distinctions will focus on diligence of effort, not ability.

The text does give some unique guidelines vital to the biblical leadership of the church. In order to understand this verse, we have to separate certain facts in the verse, evaluate them and then bring our observations together in light of the implications for the church today.

Note first that again, as is the New Testament pattern, we have elders (plural) who are serving this Ephesian church (singular). Even in this text which will give guidelines for differentiating among elders, there is still a plurality in each distinct group.

The Greek word "direct" is *prohistemi*. It is the same word used earlier in 1 Timothy 3:4 in relation to an elder's family. The word is used in Greek literature to speak of one who is a champion, protector, leader, or manager. The imagery is one who has run the race, or is setting the pace, in relation to the ministry. In other words, an elder in the church is to have a proven record in family life and conduct, and might also have a similar posture in ministry activities. Note that even director or manager in the text is in the plural. There is no one man who is *most* significant as a leader in the assembly, even though the verse does make a distinction among elders. While all elders are to lead or manage their families well (1 Tim. 3:4), not all elders will equally lead or manage in the church.

At this point, an interpretational generation gap might already be forming in the reader's mind. From our twentieth century perspective, we use words which can mean different things to different people. Remembering that this verse is *the* verse most often used by traditional church leaders to justify a unique or special position over other "lay" elders, those men might over-interpret their significance for the church.

We can conclude that while all men are to be equally qualified in relation to family, some will be distinct in ministry tasks outside the home. Such elders of distinction "are worthy of double honor." All elders are worthy of single honor in the assembly — that is recognition for status and service (cf. "honor" in relation to women in 1 Tim. 5:3, and elders in 5:17ff) — but, some elders are worthy of an additional, or double, honor of financial compensation for their labor (5:18).

Two important observations follow from the latter part of the text. First, the Greek for "work" is *kopos*, which means to labor or toil. Emphasis is on the effort taken to accomplish a task. Paul recommends that the elders are to recognize the need for a remunerative schedule that appreciates the extra labor expended to accomplish ministry tasks.

In the New Testament churches utilized plurality of elders, together shepherding the flock. This means they were ministering to the sick (James 5:14), admonishing and teaching (1 Thess. 5:12–13; Heb. 13:7), and guarding the flock against error (Acts 20:28, 1 Pet. 5:1–2). They ministered to individuals, small groups, and believers who gathered regularly.

As these elders served the church, certain ones surfaced as working harder in the ministry. The distinction was not based on gifts or abilities, but on diligence of labor. From Ken's experience, on a basketball team, all five players dribble, pass, and shoot. But certain players go all out. It is obvious to those who know the game, that regardless of the level of ability required to play, some players are more intense that others. They simply work harder. Just as extra effort is rewarded on the court, so it is to be rewarded in the church.

There is a second observation to be made. The English translation "especially those whose work is preaching and teaching" is somewhat confusing. The double honor seems to be reserved for *the* preacher. This fits with the practice in most churches today. But the better translation would be "especially those who labor in the word [*logos*] and doctrine [*didaskalia*]." The word "word" is a verbalization of truth, while the word "doctrine" is the internalization of a system of thought or teaching. The former is what one says; the latter is what one thinks. "Doctrine" issues into "word." These two words are combined in the same manner in 1 Timothy 4:6; 6:3; 2 Timothy 4:2–3; Titus 1:9; and Titus 2:7–8.

The verse does not, translated correctly, distinguish between laymen and real elders—ones who preach at the church meetings and perform the spiritual responsibilities associated with shepherding the flock. Distinctions among elders come from differences of effort, not ability.

Based on the list of qualifications for all elders from 1 Timothy 3 and Titus 1, *each* was responsible to study and understand the word of God (2 Tim. 2:15; Titus 1:9) in order to teach (1 Tim. 3:2; 2 Tim. 2:2, 24) in the church. Our twentieth-century Sunday meetings "prove" that only some of our church leadership —namely "the pastor(s)"—study and teach the Word. But in the first century, and from the New Testament, we see that *every* elder was responsible for studying and teaching believers in the assembly. Consequently, the focus of 1 Timothy 5:17 is a distinction based not on a preaching ministry, but rather based on the intensity of effort spent to accomplish the same tasks.

As the church responds with the financial support that the diligent ones deserve, these men are able to do two things: 1) continue to do what they are doing; and 2) have a teaching and modeling effect on both the body and the other leaders. They are demonstrating, by their lives, what is the high and commendable task of pastoral care. They function as resource staff who teach other leaders how to serve with similar diligence.

Yet it is at this point where some of the greatest mistakes of church leadership are made. Due to a Christian leader's educational credentials, ministry reputation, or even experience, a church will apply corporation mentality and place this man (or men) over other leaders. The church asks a man to do the shepherding that all of the elders are responsible to do. That is the mistake. But a biblical ministry of shepherding by any man is always limited. Every man can maintain only so many relationships—outside his necessary commitments to his wife and family. The key point of the verse is that the church is to let these diligent elders do their job well by giving them the time to minister, rather than making them support themselves and their families. Let those men do their jobs well—and most effectively—and let all the elders continue to shepherd the flock. To misconstrue that text is to overwork a few and deprive the assembly from the combined ministry and wisdom of all the elders who are to pastor and teach the flock.

First Timothy 5:17 remains a strategic verse for the shaping of a biblical philosophy of leadership. It cannot be used as an exegetical club to bludgeon all other passages into submission, but neither can it be disregarded. Acknowledging differences among elders based on diligence rather than extra-biblical credentials reaffirms the New Testament conclusions that there really is only one type of elder.

Equality does not mean sameness among elders any more than in the Body of Christ. A wise church will be able to both recognize the contributions of its individual leaders and hold up all the elders as valuable shepherds given to them by God for the body's welfare. Of course, it also follows that leaders in the church equally understand these principles!

LEADERSHIP: BUILDING UP ONE MAN, OR ONE ANOTHER

The Scriptures speak with forthrightness in matters of leadership and ministry. Issuing from our Lord's model of ministry in Matthew 20, several New Testament authors reaffirm the fact that the church is to be led by men who shepherd the flock of God. The following conclusions follow from these texts.

First, biblical church leadership embraces the dual principles of plurality and parity. A church is to be led by a group, not by an individual. In this group, or board, all are equal. No vote or contribution becomes, by itself, determinative. Each man recognizes a responsibility to contribute to the shepherding of the assembly; he also recognizes the value of *each* other man on that board for contributions and decisions. Although current opinions differ on matters of consensus, we have always believed that unanimity is appropriate for decision-making on the board. If God has brought a man into church leadership, though his dissenting opinion might be a minority opinion, we are committed to waiting for genuine consensus before moving ahead. It may be slower, but we have found it to be honoring to the Lord in our assemblies. This principle of unanimity is less clear in the Scriptures, though, than the principles of plurality and parity.

Second, biblical church leadership is one among, not one over. An elder or pastor in the church is not the quarterback or the head coach. He is a player-coach among other player-coaches. He is a member of the body. He also has additional responsibilities for which he is accountable. But he leads by serving and by guarding the parity of the board.

There is a well-kept secret going through Wall Street. A number of Fortune 500 Corporations have been experimenting with what they call "presidential teams." That is, they are recognizing that the demands of a corporation on one man may not be the most profitable way to run a business. Someone ought to tell the church. Why is it that in a recent survey, one out of every four pastors is discouraged and ready to quit? In major part, it has to be the demand put on him by the church or by himself, that he has to be super-minister. That does not work in the church. It might not even be working in corporations.

Third, biblical church leadership is able to emphasize unique personal contributions. There is a difference between parity and parrotry. Equality is not sameness. The New Testament recognizes the need for diligence associated with the ministry. It provides recommendations for compensation based on the labor and time requirements of ministry tasks. Yet even these decisions should be made corporately by the leadership and not through individual assessment alone. Plurality of elders does not result in a uniform "Polly want a cracker!"

BIBLICAL PRINCIPLES OF
FEMALE LEADERSHIP AND MINISTRY

Before finishing the subject of leadership, it would be inappropriate not to add some observations about the place of women in the church. Recognizing that books have been written on this subject and that we have less room here, nevertheless some general observations and two pertinent New Testament passages are in order.

There are currently only two men who do not appreciate

women. One of them is dead, and the other one is not yet born. It would be folly to diminish the value and importance of womanhood. In the Old Testament Eve is received by Adam with a joyous shout. Sarah becomes a model godly woman. Zipporah is a woman of courage and quick mind. Miriam brought praise to Yahweh along with Moses. Deborah judged among the nations. Ruth and Esther became examples of spiritual resolve. Widows carry a special place as well.

In the gospels, who are the stable followers of the Lord? Who understand the implications of His teachings on His death? Who provided the support and worship? Who were the first to the tomb? Who is the supreme model of giving and of prayer? It was again women. So it would be pure folly to demean the value of women in both life and ministry.

Given that backdrop, two important passages offer guidelines for leadership and ministry for women. The first is by way of prohibition, the second by way of prescription.

1 Timothy 2:12–14

> I do not permit a woman to teach or to have authority over a man; she must be silent. For Adam was formed first, then Eve. And Adam was not the one deceived; it was the woman who was deceived and became a sinner.

In this chapter Paul begins to give guidelines to both men and women concerning proper conduct in the church (1 Tim. 2:8–11). In his letter to Timothy at Ephesus, he gives a clear principle. Women are not to teach or exercise authority over a man. What does this mean? From other word usages, we can conclude that, at least, it means that a woman is not to do the kind of teaching to men that Timothy is commanded to do (1 Tim. 4:11; 6:1–2). That is, when dealing with major doctrines of the church, it is the place of men to teach men. Any activity or responsibility given to a woman that violates this principle is wrong. Likewise, the authority that accompanies the teaching of male leadership is not to be given to women. Although some church situations are less clear, such as when a boy becomes a man, and some Scriptures are hard to place in relation to this principle (cf. 1 Cor. 11:5 with 14:34), nevertheless the principle is clear.

The reasons for this principle are two-fold. The first is the order of creation (1 Tim. 2:13). We should understand and believe this prohibition because of the fact that Adam was created first and then Eve. Even a casual reading of Genesis 2 supports this conclusion. Second, from the order of deception (1 Tim. 2:14). Now whether it is because of vulnerability or as a judgment for Eve's conduct in Genesis 3, women are not to have a place of teaching or authority over a man. The first reason is pre-Fall. The second is post-Fall. Both are supracultural. They tell us that there are boundaries to a woman's ministry in the church that are as applicable today as they were in the first century.

Titus 2:3–5

> Likewise, teach the older women to be reverent in the way they live, not to be slanderers or addicted to much wine, but to teach what is good. Then they can train the younger women to love their husbands and children, to be self-controlled and pure, to be busy at home, to be kind, and to be subject to their husbands, so that no one will malign the work of God.

In the book of Titus, commonly referred to as the "Epistle of Good Works," Paul writes concerning ministry guidelines. In many senses the book is parallel to 1 Timothy. Paul gives Titus things to teach the older men, the younger men, the older women— then he stops. Truths that must be taught the younger women are to be taught by the older women. It seems Paul understands that men have a particular inability to communicate to young women matters vital to marriage, ministry, and godliness. That is to be the job of older women. Further, this is such a worthy ministry task that Paul notes that success at this ministry level will have a direct bearing on the attitudes people have about the Scriptures.

What are the implications of the truths in this passage? In our judgment, men are unable to minister effectively and regularly to women in the way that women are. The last time we checked, the Body of Christ was at least half women. That means that there are major ministry opportunities available for women in the church.

It follows directly from that that there should be staff positions available for women of proved spiritual character in the church. If they are to minister, they need time. That would seem to mean that, unless support comes from a husband or others, it should come from the assembly. Likewise, it seems that churches should respect these servants and co-laborers in the same sense that Paul commended Phoebe (Rom. 16:1).

We have done a double disservice to women in the church in the past. First we have at times given them teachings and seminars which simply say, "Go get 'em. You can do it. The world—and the church—is waiting!" But that is simply not true and not fair. It is not true in that churches do not yet value women as they should. It is not fair unless guidelines and boundaries for ministry, from the Scripture, are equally given.

The second disservice is that we have said at times the opposite of "Go!" We have said, "Stop!" But what does stop mean? We have emphasized 1 Timothy 2:12 without mentioning the Phoebes and the Aquila and Priscilla teams. Scripture is not interested in shouting "Stop" to women. Rather, it says, to both men and women, "If you desire ministry and leadership, that's good (1 Tim. 2:9–10; 3:1). Now plan out your efforts within the prohibitions and prescriptions of the New Testament."

The issue at hand concerning the place of women in the church is not ability. If we were to choose our pastor based strictly on communication ability, we would choose . . . Ethel Barrett! Talk about communication! But the issue is the principles of maleness and femaleness laid down form the Garden of Eden to the guidelines for Ephesus. The task of the church is both to believe the guidelines and to hold up our women who co-labor in leadership and ministry as valuable and worthy parts of the Body of Christ.

CONCLUSIONS

A farmer can contain his cows with an electric fence. Though the wires are small, they pack a wallop! When the wires are removed so that the cows can move from one pasture to another, they always balk. In fact, it is sometimes practically impossible to drive them through the opening. Though the obstacle, namely the wire, is no longer there, they rely on habit and fear to resist being moved.

So it is in the church. The fence is down. It packed a wallop called tradition and habit. There is now no reason that God's people—leaders and members of the body—should not go through it. There may still be some fear. But, some have gone through; others are considering it. Don't be left behind!

9

Spiritual Gifts
for the Church

"The greatest task of your Christian experience is discovering, and using, your spiritual gift." Sound familiar? Such is the message of books on the subject of spiritual gifts. Today you can sign up for week-long seminars or fill in long questionnaires that guarantee an ability to discover your God-given, but previously unknown, spiritual ability.

Again we see that confusion exists at the definitional level:

- A spiritual gift is a God given ability for service (C. C. Ryrie).
- A spiritual gift is a natural capacity of the individual that God has reworked for spiritual good and service (Anonymous).
- A spiritual gift denotes extraordinary gifts of the Holy Spirit dwelling and working in a special manner in individuals (Herman Cremer).

Those definitions, which span almost a hundred years of biblical research, leave many questions unanswered: Are spiritual gifts unique to the Christian experience? Is there an individual, residual capacity that God takes, and remakes? Can gifts be manifested outside the service of the church? How do you discover your gift(s)?

Further, why is it that, in the teachings of some of our most noted Christian leaders (who have had years of experience with the subject in their congregations), that significant confusion continues to exist? Why is there is no clear formula for discovering your gift? It seems that the New Testament assemblies had little problem knowing what gifts they had. Their problem was taking those known gifts and using them in a proper manner. That manner of thinking on gifts has been somewhat forgotten. Some clarification would be helpful.

DISTRIBUTIONS OF SPIRITUAL GIFTS

Apart from the New Testament passages dealing with the problems associated with the exercise of gifts in the churches, we must focus on five New Testament passages that feature gift lists:

> To one there is given through the Spirit the message of wisdom, to another the message of knowledge by means of the same Spirit, to another faith by the same Spirit, to another gifts of healing by that one Spirit, to another miraculous powers, to another prophecy, to another the ability to distinguish between spirits, to another the ability to speak in different kinds of tongues, and to still another the interpretation of tongues. (1 Cor. 12:8–10)

> And in the church God has appointed first of all apostles, second prophets, third teachers, then workers of miracles, also those having gifts of healing, those able to help others, those with gifts of administration, and those speaking in different kinds of tongues. Are all apostles? Are all prophets? Are all teachers? Do all work miracles? Do all have gifts of healing? Do all speak in tongues? Do all interpret? But eagerly desire the greater gifts. (1 Cor. 12:28–31)

> We have different gifts, according to the grace given us. If a man's gift is prophesying, let him use it in proportion to his faith. If it is serving, let him serve; if it is teaching, let him teach; if it is encouraging, let him encourage; if it is contributing to the needs of others, let him give generously; if it is leadership, let him govern diligently; if it is showing mercy, let him do it cheerfully. (Rom. 12:6–8)

> It was he who gave some to be apostles, some to be prophets, some to be evangelists, and some to be pastors and teachers. (Eph. 4:11)

> Each one should use whatever gift he has received to serve others, faithfully administering God's grace in its various forms. If anyone speaks, he should do it as one speaking the very words of God. If

BIBLICAL PHILOSOPHY OF MINISTRY

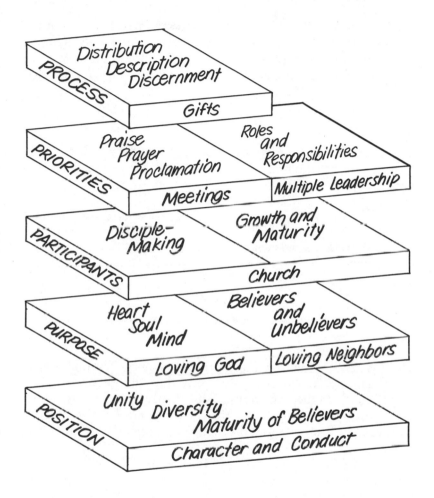

Figure 7

anyone serves, he should do it with the strength God provides, so that in all things God may be praised through Jesus Christ. To him be the glory and the power for ever and ever. Amen. (1 Pet. 4:10–11)

Those passages introduce us to the many manifestations of the Spirit's work in the body. The gifts include men as well as ministries and public as well as private services. We shall now make some initial observations to help us set the stage for specific inquiry.

CHURCH GROWTH BEGINS WITH UNITY

In each of the four epistles that record the gift lists, body maturity begins with unity. In 1 Corinthians, Paul strongly emphasizes that point:

There are different kinds of gifts, but the same Spirit. There are different kinds of service, but the same Lord. There are different kinds of working, but the same God works all of them in all men. (1 Cor. 12:4–6)

But God has combined the members of the body and has given greater honor to the parts that lacked it, so that there should be no division in the body, but that its parts should have equal concern for each other. (1 Cor. 12:24b–25)

There is no question that God's priority is unity. The diversity of gifts has a special place in the body, but the gifts are not to distract us from the same Spirit. Paul clearly points out that God Himself has lifted up in honor the "lacking parts" of the body for two reasons: first, to avoid divisions and second, to insure equal concern.

Similarly, Paul begins passages in other epistles with the same emphasis. In Romans, he states that "just as each of us has one body with many members, and these members do not all have the same function, so in Christ we who are many form one body" (12:4–5a). In Ephesians, the grace gifts given by the ascended Lord are "to prepare God's people for works of service, so that the body of Christ may be built up until we all reach unity in the faith" (4:12–13a). Peter reminds us in his first epistle that believers, "like living stones, are being built into a spiritual house to be a holy priesthood. . . . You are the people of God" (1 Pet. 2:5, 10). Unity precedes diversity.

We can safely conclude that any stress on the issue of spiritual gifts that fractures rather than heals, or separates rather than binds, or uplifts rather than promotes oneness, is inappropriate and imbalanced. As we saw in chapter 3, the very essence of the gospel has brought all believers into one body—without division or distinction. Gifts do not change that truth.

CHURCH GROWTH REQUIRES UNITY AND DIVERSITY

Oneness is not sameness. As illustrated by the character of the Trinity—unity can include diversity. The Body of Christ likewise is one, though its parts are many. Just as it would be folly for a physician not to evaluate a patient's physical problems according to the health of his organs, muscles, blood, and so on, so also would it be equally inefficient for us to evaluate the life of the Body of Christ without some appreciation of its constituent parts. Diversity is formed from the ground up:

> Consequently, you are no longer foreigners and aliens, but fellow citizens with God's people and members of God's household, built on the foundation of the apostles and prophets, with Christ Jesus himself as the chief cornerstone. (Eph. 2:19–20)

> By the grace God has given me, I laid a foundation as an expert builder, and someone else is building on it. But each one should be careful how he builds. (1 Cor. 3:10)

The apostles and the prophets laid the foundation of the church, namely Christ. The builders are distinct from the foundation, in that they have become the *temple* of God (1 Cor. 3:16; Eph. 2:21).

A physical body is the sum of its cellular parts; so the Body of Christ is the sum of its individual parts: the eye needs the hand, and the head needs the feet. And *each* part of the body needs every other part (1 Cor. 12:14–22)!

CHURCH GROWTH BRINGS MATURITY

In chapter 3, we developed an overview of the character and conduct of the church. We established that we are "members together of one body," and that the work of the ministry is "speaking the truth in love, [so that] we will in all things grow up into him who is the Head, that is, Christ" (Eph. 3:6; 4:15). Church growth is not primarily involved with numerical growth, but with spiritual growth. Geographic and numerical expansion was a result of spiritual nurture within the New Testament assemblies. The church operates correctly when it understands who it is in Christ and what it is to do in Christ.

Maturity. Growing *into* Christ. Four observations from Ephesians 4 help put this into perspective.

First, maturity is service.

> . . . to prepare God's people for works of service, so that the body of Christ may be built up. (v. 12)

Earlier Paul had written forcefully that each of us is saved by grace through faith, and that this salvation is to result in good works (Eph. 2:8–10). Continuing this thrust, he reminds his readers that the diverse gifts of grace given to the Body have a unified function: they all produce service. Just as a pot or bowl is shaped with a purpose in mind, even so believers are saved with service in mind. James's solution to pure religion included, in part, a pouring out of a believer's energies into the needs of widows and orphans in distress (James 1:27). This is genuine religion. It is the leadership and the body cooperating to serve the needs of those around us. "And the second is like it: 'Love your neighbor as yourself' " (Matt. 22:39).

Second, maturity is sanctification.

> . . . attaining to the whole measure of the fullness of Christ (v. 13).

When Christ rose from the dead, He established His final dominion over all things and initiated the doctrines of the Body of Christ (vv. 18–23). The church is both positionally the fullness of Christ and relationally moving toward that final sanctification. When our unity in the faith, our knowledge of the Son of God, and our measure of Christ's fullness all come together, then we are mature. Needless to say, maturity is not instantly gained.

Third, maturity is stability.

> Then we will no longer be infants, tossed back and forth by the waves, and blown here and there by every wind of teaching and

by the cunning and craftiness of men in their deceitful scheming
(v. 14).

The naivete of children—not only are children full of questions,
but almost any answer will do. So it is with spiritual infants. Any
new wind of teaching can sidetrack them from major issues of
ministry and growth. Spiritual maturity cannot occur without
doctrine; it protects from danger, and provides a framework for
growth.

Fourth, maturity is supportive.

> From him the whole body, joined and held together by every
> supporting ligament, grows and builds itself up in love, as each part
> does its work. (v. 16)

One major objective in John's classes is helping students appreciate
the finer things in life, namely, the Dallas Cowboys! There is a
regular ritual. If the Cowboys lose on Sunday there is a guar-
anteed quiz the following week. If they win, then there is only
a possibility of a quiz. It is amazing how that generates fan
support! If the Cowboys, with all their individual talents, did
not work together as a team, the result would be disastrous.
Likewise, the "name of the game" in body growth is cooperation.
As each part does its work, then the body is growing. Maturity is
developing.

DESCRIPTIONS OF SPIRITUAL GIFTS

Spiritual gifts are distributions of grace by Christ and the
Spirit. They are given to us for our individual and corporate
growth. The identifications and distinctions among these abilities
are as follows:

GIFT	PASSAGE	IDENTIFICATION
Apostle (*apostolos*)	1 Cor. 12:28 1 Cor. 12:29–30 Eph. 4:11	The basic meaning of the term *apostle* is a "sent one." This word, however, is used in the New Testament in two distinctive ways: (1) The term is used in a restrictive manner to identify those men who were

GIFT	PASSAGE	IDENTIFICATION
		sent by Christ to lay the foundation of the church (Eph. 2:20). Thus, the restrictive use of this word refers to an *office* that was filled by those who were selected, appointed, and commissioned by Christ Himself to lay the infant church's foundation. Acts 1:22 presents partial, recognizable criteria for holding that office. This office is in view when the term *apostle* is used in reference to a gift given to the church. The need for this corporate gift ended with the establishment of the early church.

(2) The term is used in a general manner to designate those men who were *sent by a church* to testify of Christ (Acts 14:14) or to perform functions to meet the needs of individuals in the church (Phil. 2:25). |
| Apostleship (*apostole*) | Rom. 1:5
 1 Cor. 9:2
 Gal. 2:8–9 | This gift was given to the ones who were in turn given to the church as apostles. It, therefore, refers to the individual gift which was given to those who would be the corporate gift (office). Like the other gifts, apostleship could be perceived and recognized, and the recipient of this gift functioned in the related office (Gal. 2:9). This gift relates to the establishment of the early church (Eph. 2:20). |
| Prophet (*prophetes*) | 1 Cor. 12:28
 1 Cor. 12:29–30
 Eph. 4:11 | This New Testament gift to the church (corporate gift) corresponds to the Old Testament prophet in that both received special, direct revelation from God concerning both predictions about the future and principles for godly living in the present. The message of a New Testament prophet could contain both aspects as he would speak for God under |

GIFT	PASSAGE	IDENTIFICATION
		the influence of the Holy Spirit. The primary responsibility of the prophet in the first century was the establishment of the infant church's foundation (Eph. 2:20).
Prophecy (*propheteia*)	Rom. 12:3–8 1 Cor. 12:8–10	This is the individual gift which each prophet (corporate gift) was given by God so that he could function in that office. The message of the prophet edified, encouraged, and comforted the church (1 Cor. 14:3).
Evangelist (*evangelistes*)	Eph. 4:11	This office (corporate gift) has as its responsibility the proclamation of the good news of Jesus Christ. This term is only used three times in the New Testament (Acts 21:8; Eph. 4:11; and 2 Tim. 4:5). Philip is the only person designated as an evangelist (Acts 21:8); however, the term *herald* (*kerux*) seems to refer to this same office (1 Tim. 2:7; 2 Tim. 1:11). In the book of Acts, the ministry of the one who was given this gift was directed toward unbelievers and was itinerant in nature.
Evangelism	None	Both the office of the apostle and prophet, as well as the pastor-teacher which will be discussed next, had corresponding individual gifts that were given to those who held those offices (corporate gifts). Even though not mentioned in the New Testament, a gift that corresponded to the office of evangelist is required. From the book of Acts, this gift involves the proclamation, or heralding, of the good news of Jesus Christ. It is the responsibility of every believer to participate in evangelism, but the one who was given this gift had a unique ability for the proclamation of salvation in Christ. This is evident

GIFT	PASSAGE	IDENTIFICATION
		when the church, except for the apostles, was scattered from Jerusalem in Acts 8. Philip, the evangelist (Acts 21:8), heralded (*kerusso*) Christ, but the rest of the church declared (*euangelizo*) the word (Acts 8:4–5).
Pastor-Teacher (*poimen-didaskalos*)	Eph. 4:11	The responsibilities of those who hold this office are leading, feeding, and protecting the church. All three responsibilities are intrinsic in the term *pastor* which means "shepherd." However, this particular combination of words and their relationship to the function of the elder/bishop suggest an emphasis on the leading and teaching responsibilities of this office.
Leading (*prohistemi*)	Rom. 12:3–8	This term is used only eight times in the New Testament. Five times the term is used with reference to the function of those who lead the church (1 Thess. 5:12; 1 Tim. 3:4; 5:12, 17). Twice it refers to the "maintaining" of good works (Tit. 3:8, 14), and once it refers to a gift or ability for service to be used within the church (Rom. 12:8). The term means "to stand before," and is the portrait of a shepherd guiding and caring for the sheep. In chapter eight, this gift was seen in relation to leadership in the church (1 Tim. 5:17).
Teaching (*didasko*)	Rom. 12:3–8 1 Cor. 12:28 1 Cor. 12:29–30	Teaching is the ability to communicate the truth of the Scriptures in a manner that brings clarification or conviction. In the New Testament, teaching involves both instructing and modeling the Word of God (1 Cor. 4:16; Phil. 3:17; 4:9). This term is used in two distinctive ways in the New Testament:

GIFT	PASSAGE	IDENTIFICATION
		(1) The term is used in a restrictive manner in reference to those who were responsible to teach in order to equip the body (Eph. 4:11; James 3:1; 2 Tim. 1:11). These individuals held the office of teacher.
		(2) The term is used in a general manner to address the responsibility of every believer (Matt. 28:20; Heb. 5:12) to teach those further behind them in their pilgrimage, at least in the foundational teachings of the Word (Heb. 6:1–2).
Exhorting (*purakaleo*)	Rom. 12:3–8	Akin to the term *paraclete* ("one called to the support of another"), this gift involves coming alongside another to help. Comfort, encouragement, as well as admonishment, are the means by which this gift may be used within the body.
Giving (*metadidomi*)	Rom 12:3 8	Only used five times in the New Testament. This gift involves the sharing or imparting of one's material possessions for the benefit of others in the body.
Showing Mercy (*eleeo*)	Rom. 12:3–8	The gift of showing mercy is the ability to manifest pity and compassion to those who are in need.
Word of Wisdom (*logos/ sophia*)	1 Cor. 12:8–10	This gift involves the translation of biblical truth into practical living. Application of the Word is in view.
Word of Knowledge (*logos/ gnosis*)	1 Cor. 12:8–10	The gift involves the accumulation of facets of truth into a systematic structure, resulting from study. Understanding the Word is in view.

GIFT	PASSAGE	IDENTIFICATION
Faith (*pistis*)	1 Cor. 12:8–10	The gift of faith is the ability to trust the Provider amidst a problem or need. Focus is placed upon the resource, not the problem.
Gifts of Healing (*charisma/ iama*)	1 Cor. 12:8–10 1 Cor. 12:28 1 Cor. 12:29–30	This gift involves the ability to restore another to health.
Operation of Powers (*energena/ dynamics*)	1 Cor. 12:8–10 1 Cor. 12:28 1 Cor. 12:29–30	The ability to perform supernatural signs and miracles is the essence of the gift.
Discerning of Spirits (*diakriss/ pneuma*)	1 Cor. 12:8–10	The gift involves the ability to determine the source of another's speech or action.
Kinds of Tongues (*genos/ glossa*)	1 Cor. 12:8–10 1 Cor. 12:28 1 Cor. 12:29–30	The gift of tongues is generally regarded as the ability to speak in a known language that has not been learned by the one who speaks.
Interpretation of tongues (*hermeneia/ glossa*)	1 Cor. 12:8–10 1 Cor. 12:29–30	The interpretation of tongues is the ability to translate the foreign language spoken by one who possessed the gift of tongues into an understandable language.
Helping (*antilempsis*)	1 Cor. 12:28	This gift involves the rendering of assistance or supporting of another in need.
Administration (*kubernesis*)	1 Cor. 12:28	The gift of administration is the ability to direct others.
Serving (*diaknos*)	Rom. 12:3–8	This gift involves meeting the needs of others.

Spiritual gifts are a lot like a diamond. As beautiful as the stone is, you cannot fully appreciate it from just one angle. You have to change the angle—catch the light in different refractions—in order to fully appreciate its beauty. Similarly, you have to see the different parts— coordinated and working together—in order to fully appreciate the spiritual gifts. A foot or hand severed from the body has no use. But in all the body parts working together is beauty.

THE CHALLENGE: DISCERNMENT AND DISCOVERY

Have you ever listened to the teaching of someone who was self-convinced that he had the gift of teaching but somehow had trouble convincing others? Maybe he did have the gift of teaching—and you just did not have the gift of listening. We have found that believers determine their gifts according to many factors. For example, personal experiences and desires, and insights and encouragement from other members of the body. Within a church organized according to this biblical blueprint, there will be a number of small group and informal settings where believers will minister and be ministered to. Elders and other believers can then be available to help a person evaluate his strengths and abilities.

It is important to note that the majority of gifts listed in this chapter are also given in similar fashion as commands for the believer. For example, concerning evangelism: "Do the work of an evangelist" (2 Tim. 4:5); leading: "Our people must learn to devote themselves to doing what is good" (Titus 3:14a); teaching: "Therefore go and make disciples . . . teaching them to obey everything I have commanded you" (Matt. 28:19a, 20a). The point is that we are to be obedient to the Scriptures whether or not we are sure about what gift(s) we may possess.

THE CULMINATION:
GIFTS THAT RESULT IN RELATIONSHIPS

We have already seen that the church is to be moving toward unity as a local body and as a part of the Body of Christ. Now it also must be said that gifts are not to be seen as an end in themselves. How we function as parts of the Body of Christ is measured in terms of our mutual concerns and affections for one another.

PASSAGE	CONTENT
John 13:34	"Love one another"
John 15:17	"Love each another"
Rom. 12:10	"Be devoted to one another"
Rom. 12:10	"Honor one another"
Rom. 12:16	"Live in harmony with one another"
Rom. 13:8	"Love one another"
Rom. 14:13	"Let us stop passing judgment on one another"
Rom. 14:19	"Mutual edification"
Rom. 15:5	"Spirit of unity among yourselves"
Rom. 15:7	"Accept one another"
Rom. 15:14	"Instruct one another"
Rom. 16:16	"Greet one another"
1 Cor. 11:33	"Wait for each other"
1 Cor. 12:25	"Concern for each other"
1 Cor. 16:20	"Greet one another"
2 Cor. 13:12	"Greet one another"
Gal. 5:13	"Serve one another"
Gal. 6:2	"Carry each other's burdens"
Eph. 4:2	"Bearing with one another in love"
Eph. 4:32	"Be kind and compassionate to one another"
Eph. 5:21	"Submit to one another"
Phil. 2:3	"Consider others better than yourselves"
Col. 3:9	"Do not lie to each other"
Col. 3:13	"Bear with each other"
1 Thess. 3:12	"Make your love increase and overflow for each other"
1 Thess. 4:9	"Love each other"
1 Thess. 4:18	"Encourage each other"
1 Thess. 5:11	"Encourage one another"
1 Thess. 5:15	"Always try to be kind to each other"
Heb. 10:24	"Spur one another"
James 4:11	"Do not slander one another"
James 5:9	"Don't grumble against each other"
James 5:16	"Confess your sins to each other"
James 5:16	"Pray for each other"
1 Pet. 1:22	"Love one another"
1 Pet. 4:9	"Offer hospitality to one another"
1 Pet. 5:5	"Clothe yourselves with humility toward one another"
1 Pet. 5:14	"Greet one another"

PASSAGE	CONTENT
1 John 3:11	"Love one another"
1 John 3:23	"Love one another"
1 John 4:7	"Love one another"
1 John 4:11	"Love one another"
1 John 4:12	"Love each other"
2 John 5	"Love one another"

The things we teach, the way we speak to one another, the financial and personal support we give, the mercy and faith we express —all are part of body building.

CONCLUSIONS

In the study of spiritual gifts *balance* is vital. There is a sense of de-emphasis of gifts in the epistles—they are not to be exulted in, or pursued, or desired for public performance. Rather, we must care for, and serve, one another in obedience to the Scriptures. We must also recognize that the Body of Christ will not grow without the exercise of its abilities for the maturity of its cellular parts. Both are true—at the same time.

10

Biblical Education
in the Home and the Church

We discovered in the first chapters what kind of modern pressures face the pastor and the Christian home in the twentieth century. Before the turn of the decade, nine out of ten mothers will be working outside the home. One study suggested that on the average, the typical father spends less than a minute a day with his preschool children. Needless to say, the challenge to the church is great.

What is the intent of God for the educational process in both the home and the church? How is the husband to be a principal teacher for his wife and children? How can the church encourage parents to be good teachers in their homes and *then* good teachers of the Body of Christ?

To this point we have been rediscovering a biblical blueprint for the church. After establishing the dilemma of the typical traditional approach to ministry (Section 1), we built a new biblical framework for evaluating the church. This included a refocusing on the character and conduct of the church: the centrality of relationships in any ministry and the guidelines for ministry modeled by Christ and the apostles (Section 2). Having overviewed the church from that perspective, we have focused on the nature of the New Testament church organization—in both its meeting and its leadership structure. In addition, the gifted ministry of the body to its individual parts has been analyzed (Section 3). It still remains for us, though, to evaluate the teaching-learning process—the process of education and indoctrination that is vital for the church to continue to meet the challenges it faces. An evaluation of the education process in the Scriptures is always twofold: first, the concern for spiritual growth in the home; and second, subsequent to the first, the spiritual growth in the community of believers. These concerns will be evaluated from both the teaching and learning perspective.

BIBLICAL TEACHING: THE MODEL AND METHOD

Does the typical approach to education in the church ever amuse you? We remember being instructed on the inefficiencies of the lecture method—through a lecture! It surprised us when we first realized that 95 percent of all pastoral training takes place in the classroom—a place devoid of reality. Likewise, the traditional sanctuary does not fare much better. Certainly, there is a place for the teaching of doctrine. And we are convinced that the supreme value of verse-by-verse exposition of Scripture is applicable in our day and culture. But, we cannot rely on the lecture method on its own merit to change lives.

How was education performed in the nation of Israel? Young boys and girls were taught at home by their parents. When boys were old enough, they followed their fathers in a specific occupation. In the life and ministry of Christ, He selected men from several trades and taught them in the context of situations they faced. When He taught them about the kingdom of God and the kingdom of Satan, it was in the midst of actual confrontations with the adversary (Mark 1:21–28; 3:20–30). The concerns of perseverance and prosperity in the disciple's life were taught through parables common to their experiences (Mark 4:1–20, 26–34). When He asked them to develop as ministry teams apart from Him, He remained available to help them evaluate the results (Mark 6:6b–13, 30–44). There can be no education apart from life-experiences.

THE TEACHING PROCESS IN THE HOME

In matters of teaching truth in the home, God has spoken clearly. For Israel, the principal vehicle of education was instruction of the parents:

BIBLICAL PHILOSOPHY OF MINISTRY

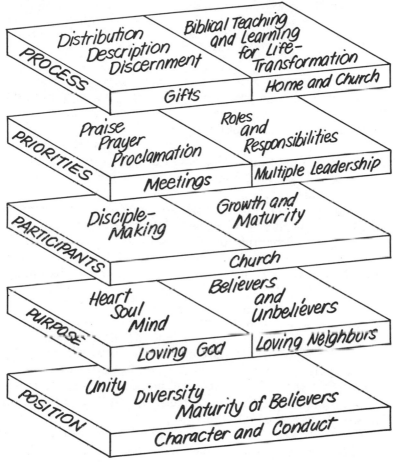

PROCESS
Distribution
Description
Discernment
Gifts

Biblical Teaching
and Learning
for Life-
Transformation
Home and Church

PRIORITIES
Praise
Prayer
Proclamation
Meetings

Roles
and
Responsibilities
Multiple Leadership

PARTICIPANTS
Disciple-Making

Growth and
Maturity
Church

PURPOSE
Heart
Soul
Mind
Loving God

Believers
and
Unbelievers
Loving Neighbours

POSITION
Unity Diversity
Maturity of Believers
Character and Conduct

Pursuing Relationships More Than Promoting
Religion

Figure 8

> Hear, O Israel: The LORD our God, the LORD is one. Love the LORD
> your God with all your heart and with all your soul and with all your
> strength. These commandments that I give you today are to be upon
> your hearts. Impress them on your children. Talk about them when
> you sit at home and when you walk along the road, when you lie down
> and when you get up. Tie them as symbols on your hands and bind
> them on your foreheads. Write them on the doorframes of your houses
> and on your gates. (Deut. 6:4–9)

In this second giving of the covenant to the new generation that
grew up while their parents suffered the discipline of God in the
wilderness, Moses points toward the need for weaving the truths
of Yahweh into the fabric of family life.

There are three stages to the teaching process. *First, biblical
teaching begins with initiation.* Based on God's uniqueness, the
Israelite parent recognized an initial responsibility to love Him
with one's total heart, soul, and strength.

There is no better starting point for spiritual transformation
than the heart. In chapter 4 we learned that "loving the Lord your
God," as quoted from this Old Testament text, was the first and
greatest commandment. All orthodoxy and orthopraxy is rooted
in that fact. If truth is dry to the heart, it is dry to the family.
There is no spiritual glaze that can fool the family. If truth is not
lived out in the home, it will not penetrate the heart.

Second, biblical teaching continues with indoctrination. There
are three ways that the text pictures indoctrination: impress, talk,
and tie. The first step is personal conviction (cf. Deut. 4:5; 6:13–19).
Then, the parent is to use opportunities and situations to transfer
these truths to the child. As we have said, the purpose of biblical
teaching is life transformation. A truth cannot be adopted without seeing how it applies to life.

In that section of Deuteronomy there is a special focus on the
son. This is typical to the Old Testament view of transmission of
truth, as the book of Proverbs repeatedly shows. Twice in
Deuteronomy 6 the son or grandsons are in view (6:2, 20; cf. 4:9).
This teaching is to be from generation to generation. The emphasis is on parental initiative, planting these truths into the lives of
the sons.

For Israel, as the fathers went, so went the sons and the nation's
future. That is graphically, yet negatively, illustrated in later Old
Testament writings. Judgment was on the generations who deserted

the faith of their fathers during the period of the Judges. Similarly, the sons of Eli, Samuel, Saul, David, and Solomon all portray the effects of neglecting the important truths of Deuteronomy 6.

Third, biblical teaching concludes with impartation. The reality that was believed and lived by the parents, and that was creatively planted in the lives of the children, blossoms into expression in the community. The message is heard, felt, and then lived out. This was the normal, though supernatural, spiritual life commanded by God in the life of the nation.

In the New Testament, a similarly central passage gives us God's pattern for parental instruction:

> Fathers, do not exasperate your children; instead, bring them up in the training and instruction of the Lord. (Eph. 6:4)

In the midst of guidelines for marital and work relationships, Paul gives the believers at Ephesus important glimpses into the home's teaching process.

First, biblical teaching comes through parental control. What we began in the Old Testament is fully affirmed in the New Testament. The key to passing biblical truth from parent to child is seen in the father. If he teaches one thing and lives another, the dry desert of Deuteronomy will be the child's experience. The Greek word for *exasperate* means literally "an angry impulse from the side." It is usually a father who teaches by intimidation and believes a strict and harsh approach will most effectively sober his children to their responsibilities (cf. Col. 3:21). But that does not work. Paul clearly states that it is not to be a part of biblical parenting and teaching.

Second, biblical teaching is corrective. The Word, when referring to children, implies reform and improvement. It stresses the importance of discipline for affirming that there are fences that the child cannot leap over without consequences. It should be said that discipline can, and should, be accomplished without anger and explosive impulses. We have tried, as parents, always to communicate to our children that we love *and* discipline them, rather than love *but* discipline them. Discipline is not inconsistent with the Lord's love for us, nor a parent's love for his child. Done correctly, it is a sign of a loving father (cf. Heb. 12:7–11).

Third, biblical teaching is instructive. Can you imagine the home where, regardless of what the child does, the father disapproves? The Greek word means "to warn." It is our word *admonish*, which means "to put (on) or influence the mind." Here the warnings and counsel of the father are given in a way to help the child avoid problems later in life. Again, this is most effective when wedded to the behavior of the father.

The biblical teaching process for the home, whether the culture is Hebrew or Greek or American, is the same. It involves the parents, accepting and believing the truths about their God, then living them out in word and deed among their families. Remember Christ's summation of the matter when He said that the greatest commandment was "love the Lord your God"; and the second is like the first, "love your neighbor as yourself!"

THE TEACHING PROCESS IN THE CHURCH

Developing teaching credentials. There are more vital questions for Christian education in the church than choice of curriculum and plans for a Sunday school rally day. In the New Testament, the teaching process was an extension of the home. The principles of personal commitment and the communication of the truth by word and life are all significant features of a teaching ministry in the church.

First Timothy's stated purpose is that "you will know how people ought to conduct themselves in God's household, which is the church of the living God, the pillar and foundation of the truth" (3:15). In chapter 3 Paul lists the qualifications for men desiring the office of overseer, or bishop. This position of elder, or pastor, carries with it the responsibilities of church leadership. In that passage and a similar one in Titus 1, we find twenty-five criteria for leadership:

CHARACTERISTIC	EXPLANATION	PASSAGE
1. Above reproach	Unquestionably of good reputation	1 Tim. 3:2
2. Husband of one wife	Adulterous attitudes, as well as relationships, in view	1 Tim. 3:2; Titus 1:6
3. Temperate	Disciplined; not in bondage to one's desires	1 Tim. 3:2
4. Sensible	Wise; observing a godly course of conduct	1 Tim. 3:2
5. Respectable	Honorable; well-ordered conduct	1 Tim. 3:2
6. Hospitable	Accepting others and willing to share with others what God has provided	1 Tim. 3:2

CHARACTERISTIC	EXPLANATION	PASSAGE
7. Able to teach	Able to communicate the truth of Scripture in a manner that brings clarification and conviction	1 Tim. 3:2; 2 Tim. 2: 24–26
8. Not given to wine	Not addicted to alcohol	1 Tim. 3:3; Titus 1:7
9. Not a striker	Not prone to physical violence	1 Tim. 3:3; Titus 1:7
10. Gentle	Forbearing; manifesting kindness	1 Tim. 3:3
11. Uncontentious	Peaceful; not quarrelsome	1 Tim. 3:3
12. Free from love of money	Not a money lover	1 Tim. 3:3
13. Leads well his own house	Leading and ruling one's family in an exceptional manner; evidencing an ability to lead the church	1 Tim. 3:4
14. Having children in subjection	Keeping one's children under control	1 Tim. 3:4; Titus 1:6
15. Not a new convert	Not spiritually immature in Christ	1 Tim. 3:6
16. Have a good witness with those outside	Personal life before unbelievers declaring the reality of Christ within; having unquestioned conduct	1 Tim. 3:7
17. Blameless	No grounds for accusation (to call to account); similar to being "above reproach"	Titus 1:6-7
18. Not self-pleasing	Not insensitive to others	Titus 1:7
19. Not quick-tempered	Not inclined to anger	Titus 1:7
20. Not fond of sordid gain	Not taking advantage of others	Titus 1:7
21. A lover of what is good	Seeking the desires of God	Titus 1:8
22. Just	Righteous; godly in conduct	Titus 1:8
23. Devout	Holy; pure in conduct	Titus 1:8
24. Self-controlled	Dominion over one's desires; similar to being "temperate"	Titus 1:8
25. Holding fast the faithful word	Knowing, living, and teaching the Word of God	Titus 1:9

Good teaching and the gift of teaching. Before all of us in church leadership fall into despair, a few observations and qualifications may help our perspective. The leader is one who is above reproach, that is, no charge made against him will be proved true. It does not mean that he, or anyone else, is perfect. James settles that matter: "Not many of you should presume to be teachers, my brothers, because you know that we who teach will be judged more strictly." Why? "We all stumble in many ways" (James 3:1–2a). At least James did not say "we all stumble in *all* ways"!

Second, this passage focuses on a man's being "able to teach." Communication skills are to be used in conjunction with other character qualities (2 Tim. 2:24–26). There are two interesting omissions in the lists of qualifications: (1) There is no direct reference to spiritual gifts as a qualification for leadership in the church. However, we do see this reference in 1 Timothy 4:14, in relation to Timothy. And (2) there is no academic or school certification for the ministry. That is especially interesting since Acts 19 speaks of the school of Tyrannus in Ephesus.

Now before we empty the halls of Bible schools and seminaries, let us explain those omissions. Paul's concern for Timothy is that men who serve in leadership should be more concerned with knowing and performing the truth than with excessive preoccupation with scholarly credentialing. If academic disciplines aid a man in developing an elder's characteristics, then he should pursue his schooling. The point is that the criteria of 1 Timothy 3 is the first and primary consideration for leadership qualification.

That does have a significant application for schools that train pastors. But, with all the curricular requirements of a pastoral program, we dare not miss the priority of life transformation: the ability of the Word of God, by the Spirit of God, to transform the servant of God.

Having said that, we are now ready to consider Paul's usage of the concept of teacher. Of the seven times Paul uses the term *teacher*, five refer to the gift or the office of teacher. In other words, the predominate usage of this term assumes a context of giftedness. As such, the gift of teaching is probably in view in 1 Timothy 3:2 and 2 Timothy 2:24. The gift of leading is also likely in view in 1 Timothy 3:4. The gift of teaching produced a teacher. The gift of leading produced a pastor (cf. 1 Tim. 3:4 with 5:17 and Rom. 12:7–8). This teacher and pastor, combined in the phrase *pastor-teacher* in Ephesians 4:11, was responsible for the household of faith.

Finally, we need to excise one word from our theological vocabulary: *layman*. That person, as an entity separate from *clergy*, does not exist in the New Testament. The word *layman* was coined in the third century when an emphasis on the head pastor, or head bishop, under Emperor Constantine, reached prominence. That position was advanced first by Ignatius, who encouraged one bishop to be over each local assembly. From that point a dichotomy developed between the "common" man, or layman, and the "professional" minister, called the bishop or clergy.

Not only does monepiscopacy, the term for that practice, ignore specific Scriptures (see chapter 8) but also the continued emphasis in second-century churches and communities that followed the plurality-of-elders design. Trained and untrained elders have no difference in parity. They are both, in the eyes of God, co-laborers in the team ministry of shepherding and instructing the flock.

SPIRITUAL MATURITY: THE LEARNING MODEL FOR LIFE TRANSFORMATION

The educational process involves both giving and receiving. There are teachers and there are learners. Remembering two former conclusions will be helpful. First, we noted in chapter 6 that the discipleship process is not a one-way ministry but a two-way mutual ministry in the body. Second, we discovered in chapter 8 that the church leader is not the quarterback but rather a player coach. He is a part of the team—a member of the body. But he also has additional responsibilities that are not applicable to the group at large.

Given those general observations, it is safe to conclude that spiritual maturity, as a learning stage in the educational process, is universally applicable in the church. The Body of Christ is a family of brothers and sisters, carrying mutual responsibilities for building up one other in the faith. As such, the need for believing and modeling those truths is again universally applicable to both leadership and the local assembly.

THE LEARNING PROCESS IN THE HOME

You can fool some of the people most of the time. You can fool most of the people some of the time. But you can't fool . . . the home! We think there are at least two reasons for Paul's recommending that leaders in the church are to be married and are to have families (cf. 1 Tim. 3). The first is that the church is a family of believers, and leadership of a family unit aids in preparing for leadership of the church (cf. 1 Tim. 3:4–5). Much is learned about pastoring by parenting!

But the second is equally practical. We think it is helpful that leaders in the church be men who are married and have been raising a family, because it reminds Dad that he is human. Gentlemen, let us face it—we are a proud lot. And it is humbling to realize regularly the need to work on our homes—on being true to one woman and on having children who "are not open to the charge of being wild and disobedient" (Titus 1:6). Yet we are convinced that the family is one of God's primary tools for shaping spiritual shepherds. Please note that as important as the home is for determining leadership qualification, nevertheless that cannot rule out single men serving as elders. If the phrase *husband of one wife* demands marriage, then the phrase *not given to much wine* demands given to a little wine. Single men are not to be excluded.

Some would say that a pastor's priorities are always changing, depending on the current demands of his family, ministry, and life-style. But, the home should have a higher priority than the church. That fact is taken from the context of 1 Timothy 3. Vocational Christian leaders make a serious mistake when they attempt to draw a parallel between a commitment to the Lord and a commitment to the ministry. Everyone must make the Lord his first priority, his family as a second priority, and all other matters, including his ministry, as a third priority. Remember, Paul clearly states that the home is a God-given barometer for measuring a man's qualification for leadership in the church: if he does not measure up in the home, then he should be disqualified for leadership service in the church (1 Tim. 3:4–5).

THE LEARNING PROCESS IN THE CHURCH

For both the leadership and the entire assembly, learning is a necessity. In relationship to leaders in the church, Paul gives us a glimpse into his philosophy of ministry and learning:

> Brothers loved by God, we know that he has chosen you, because our gospel came to you not simply with words, but also with power, with the Holy Spirit and with deep conviction. You know how we lived among you for your sake. You became imitators of us and of the Lord;

in spite of severe suffering, you welcomed the message with the joy given by the Holy Spirit. And so you became a model to all the believers in Macedonia and Achaia. (1 Thess. 1:4–7)

There are three spiritual learning generations in this passage. First, there is the learner Paul. His ministry emphases included a confidence in the gospel and in the Holy Spirit. But he also says, "You know how we lived among you for your sake." Like the toy rabbit's experience in the children's classic *The Velveteen Rabbit*, being real requires hard work. Your fuzz gets worn off; your ears droop; one eye might even pop out. But that is part of life. Likewise, Paul lived or literally "came to be" among these believers. There is nothing that motivates people like the genuine article.

Second, there are the learners at Thessalonica. They heard the gospel and welcomed it with joy. They made the priorities of Paul their own, committing themselves to transparency.

Third, the message went out to Macedonia and Achaia. This life transmission, summarized in 2 Timothy 2:2, and historically visualized here, shows us the long-range perspective on learning in the church.

CONCLUSIONS

The Christian church and the Christian home are desperately looking for velveteen rabbits. In the book, the rabbit's friend was the skin horse. His advice was, "Real isn't how you are made. It's a thing that happens to you. When a child loves you for a long, long time, not just to play with, but really loves you, then you become real!"

Stretched throughout the church is a line of lives waiting for the real—to be held as the goal and to be modeled in life. These lives, young and old, are willing to commit themselves to the *real* cause of life transformation in the church. They are waiting for ones with the counsel of the skin horse and the character of the velveteen rabbit.

Section 4

Translating Theology into Practice, or How to Be Biblical Even If It Hurts

11

Transforming an Established Church

We have observed that counterfeits have always stalked the church of God—sounding fundamental but erring on matters of significance. We have seen that the true household of God finds its roots in the soil of apostolic doctrine, its structure on the foundation of Jesus Christ.

Christ, on our behalf, has initiated His church. Every ministry effort and plan—organization and credential—must answer to that foundation. The work of the Body of Christ is motivated by the mercies of Christ. Those mercies are the plan of God that has resulted in salvation by grace through faith. For those receiving Christ, they not only are now found in Christ but are joined together as members of His body. This joining, referred to as "members together of one body, and sharers together in the promise in Christ Jesus" (Eph. 3:6), is the spiritual reality that nurtures the growth of the church.

WHERE DO WE START?

There can be union without unity. If you were to take two tomcats, tie their tails together, and throw them over a clothesline, would you have union? Yes. Unity? No! So it is in the church. Today we have many denominations, organizations, and associations under the banner of Christian ministry. Yet we must

143

be most interested in genuine unity which produces a maturing body of believers. Anything less is counterfeit. It may look good, but if it defers from the New Testament model of ministry, it is defective.

Have you ever noticed how different people react to questions? Sometimes asking a question, a simple question, can create an unexpected response. When David simply asked, " . . . Who is this uncircumcised Philistine, that he should defy the armies of the living God?" (1 Sam. 17:26), the response was swift and abusive. David was attacked in two ways. First, his motive was attacked: "Why have you come down here?. . . . I know how conceited you are and how wicked is your heart; for you have come down only to watch the battle." (1 Sam. 17:28). Then his ministry was attacked: " . . . With whom did you leave those few sheep in the desert?" (1 Sam. 17:28). Quite an answer for such a simple question!

Similarly, Ken has experienced the same heated reaction, sometimes nonverbal, when asking questions that focused on the need for change. Some have even said, "If you cannot agree with this, you do not belong here," and, "Why don't you just start another church, rather than disrupting this one?" In both cases, a sincere desire to change to a more biblical model was rejected.

At the outset it is true that change is hard. There is something inside us that resists it. But we are not simply talking about changes for novelty. We are talking about improvements for the church that bring us into closer conformity with the instructions of the New Testament, which warn us, "Do not go beyond what is written" (1 Cor. 4:6). Our desire is that the true life of the church can be reestablished in a way to produce disciples and believers who are progressing steadily in their abilities to love the Lord their God and love their neighbor as themselves.

DECISION-MAKING AND THE CHURCH

For many readers there exists a lingering but substantial question: "If the church is truly a growing body of believers, designed for maturity and cooperative support, then I can see where change is needed. But, the decisions for our church are made by the congregation, not the leadership. The buildings are owned by our denomination. Changes would disrupt those who are in control— it will never happen!"

Does that sound even somewhat familiar? It is a question we

have been asked, in some form, dozens of times. There are answers and the answers are again grounded in the Scriptures:

> In those days when the number of disciples was increasing, the Grecian Jews among them complained against those of the Aramaic-speaking community because their widows were being overlooked in the daily distribution of food. So the Twelve gathered all the disciples together and said, "It would not be right for us to neglect the ministry of the word of God in order to wait on tables. Brothers, choose seven men from among you who are known to be full of the Spirit and wisdom. We will turn this responsibility over to them and will give our attention to prayer and the ministry of the word."
>
> This proposal pleased the whole group. They chose Stephen, a man full of faith and of the Holy Spirit; also Philip, Procorus, Nicanor, Timon, Parmenas, and Nicolas from Antioch, a convert to Judaism. They presented these men to the apostles, who prayed and laid their hands on them.
>
> So the word of God spread. The number of disciples in Jerusalem increased rapidly, and a large number of priests became obedient to the faith. (Acts 6:1–7)

The increasing numbers in the growing church in Jerusalem brought new demands, and the problem was brought to the attention of the apostles.

Our first concern is to notice the involvement of the apostles as leaders of the Jerusalem assembly. They gathered the disciples (Acts 6:2), formulated the plan (Acts 6:2–4), and ultimately sanctioned the men chosen to assist, by laying their hands on them (Acts 6:6). There is little question who is leading in the matter. The apostles were concerned and needed a proposal that allowed them to continue with their responsibilities. The selection of "the Seven" accomplished that objective.

On the other hand, notice the involvement of the congregation of disciples. Beyond the secondary issues of whether this was a select group known as "disciples" or whether it referred to the whole Jerusalem assembly, the major matter is the cooperation and participation of the group with the apostles. The problem was discussed with the congregation (Acts 6:2), and they were enlisted as participants in the solution (Acts 6:3). The plan was met with unanimous approval (Acts 6:5), and the ministries of those seven Greek brothers contributed to the spread of the church (Acts 6:7).

What principles, from this text, speak to the issue of decision-making and the church? *First, God had ordained leadership for the church.* Christ had predicted that His church would be built upon Peter (Matt. 16:16–18) and the apostles (Matt. 18:15–20; 19:28). As the book of Acts develops, the apostles and elders join in cooperative leadership efforts (14:23; 15:2, 4, 22). By the end of Paul's third missionary journey, as he begins his trip to Rome, the affairs of the churches are left in the care of the elders (20:17, 32–38). The ministry of the apostles and elders provided the shepherding leadership necessary for the growth of the New Testament church.

That fact is repeated. In words similar to the counsel given by Paul at Ephesus, Peter reminds the undershepherds of the churches that they are to "be shepherds of God's flock under your care" (1 Pet. 5:2). The author to the Hebrews reminds the brothers that they are to "obey your leaders and submit to their authority" (Heb. 13:17). Leadership and authority in the assembly is given to those who are called elders and overseers—men who shepherd the church.

Second, in Acts 6 God had also ordained congregations who participate in the life and needs of the church. The congregation of disciples enthusiastically cooperated with the twelve in solving the needs of the Grecian widows. Even so, a church is functioning properly when both the leadership and congregation cooperate in ministering to the needs of those around them (cf. Acts 15:2, 4, 22).

There is a parallel in the home. The head of a woman is man (1 Cor. 11:3). As the ones ultimately accountable for the nurture and growth of our families, we recognize our responsibility to lead our families in matters of spiritual growth. But we would be "full of folly" if we ignored the insights and needs of our wives. Our designated place as head is in no way a club of superiority. We are rather to recognize the equal spiritual status of our wives and live with them in a skillful manner so that our own spiritual growth can continue (1 Pet. 3:7). In a similar manner in the church, elders are to provide the kind of leadership that holds members of the body up as worthy and equal brothers in the assembly and that facilitates direction and ministry that brings corporate growth.

Third, a careful balance of loving leadership and cooperating congregations produces a growing church. There can be imbalances toward elder rule or toward congregational rule. Neither group is to use its position (elders or overseers) or its valued approval (congregation) in power struggles. The New Testament church grew and prospered because the leadership, like a husband, understood its responsibility under God to lead, and the congregation, like a wife, understood its responsibility under God to follow in an enthusiastic and participatory fashion.

Finally, unless we employ the authority of apostles today, which we cannot defend from the New Testament, the authority of any organization over the autonomy of a local assembly is indefensible. Denominations, associations, sessions, conferences, or parachurch agencies all must recognize that they exist strictly for serving the church, not overseeing it. If the authority of the apostles was transferred anywhere in the New Testament, it was transferred to the Scriptures themselves (2 Pet. 3:14–18). All too quickly denominations, organizations, or associations begin to make decisions according to vested interests rather than according to biblical criteria. If that is happening, history will record the demise of that group.

PRINCIPLES OF TRANSITION FOR THE CHURCH

We see the need for cooperation in a spirit of approval and obedience, and understand that the spiritual leadership of the church is responsible "to prepare God's people for works of service" (Eph. 4:12). Now four principles of transition are necessary for accomplishing unity and maturity in the Body.

First, the church is a flock, not a herd. The apostles repeatedly referred to believers as sheep. The flock, as a group, needs encouragement and direction, protection and feeding. Like the Good Shepherd, who becomes the model for shepherding, intimacy develops in relationships—a trust and affection born out of time spent together (John 10). A herd is driven; a flock is led. Believers who form the Body of Christ need to be cared for in matters of life and spiritual growth.

Second, the church is led by shepherds, not ranchers. Some modern church-growth theorists see the pastor as the rancher who oversees his sprawling spread and keeps count of his herd. He cares for basic needs but is certainly above the specific problems and concerns of his herd. But leadership in the church is done by shepherds—men who are pastors more than prodders. They are ones-among rather than ones-over. They are brothers in the assembly, which ultimately has only one Master (Matt. 23:8–12).

Third, the church offers pastoral services, not preaching stations. In most church circles, the decision to have multiple Sunday services is received with joy. But we suspect the enthusiasm is premature. The work of the ministry is knowing and leading the flock—encouraging cooperation and relationships through leadership modeling. If a church grows numerically to the point of needing larger facilities or outgrowing its effectiveness for ministry on a relational basis, then the proper response is real church growth—planting daughter works in a spirit of evangelism and mission—rather than cultivating enormous preaching stations.

Fourth, the church is to encourage community, not commuters. The twentieth century is an age of mobility. We are able to travel quickly from place to place with very few physical limitations. But this commuting mentality has hurt the church. Whether the reasons for believers traveling out of their community on Sunday morning relate to a popular preacher or an appealing education program, the disadvantages become quickly apparent. Significant travel time, less contact with neighbors, and an inability to coordinate church ministry and evangelistic efforts within the community all contribute to the loss of a sense of community. Needless to say, it is impossible to "love my neighbor as myself" if I only wave to him as I drive by! In the New Testament church believers and leaders intimately knew each other. They got together more than just during times of preaching and crisis-counseling. They learned how to love the Lord together and love each other as an expression of worship. They taught each other and admonished each other, remembering that the goal was maturity and that each member of the body was necessary for accomplishing that end.

On the other hand, if a local church offers the ministries that you determine are biblical and necessary, then relocation to the community where the believers live and the meetings are conducted seems reasonable and prudent.

WHAT CAN WE DO?

To the extent that our churches may deviate from the New Testament model, we need the courage to face the question, What can we do? For some churches the change may be made with small course corrections. For others it may mean the possible loss of buildings and facilities or the severance from an association that refuses to cooperate with the necessary changes.

To be realistic, most churches need more than a week of meetings and a revised constitution; the changes go much deeper than that. For most assemblies caught in traditions that cannot be defended biblically, a minimum of four years is needed to accomplish the changes of direction necessary to bring them in line with the New Testament model. The following steps provide a general blueprint which, of course, should be modified to the needs and situations of any given assembly.

PHASE ONE: CHECKING THE BLUEPRINTS

There is no motivation that can compare to doctrinal motivation. Thus, the first step for a church is evaluation and study. Evaluation allows for the expectations and needs within the church to be known, along with understanding the past contributions of the assembly. The process of study allows a church to develop a strategy for a biblical philosophy of the church. Based on the facts determined by evaluation, the extent of change necessary can be determined.

At the outset, it is worth remembering that the Bereans were highly commended in the New Testament for the following reasons:

> Now the Bereans were of more noble character than the Thessalonians, for they received the message with great eagerness and examined the Scriptures every day to see if what Paul said was true. (Acts 17:11)

Can you imagine listening to the apostle Paul and yet reserving an opinion until you have had the time to study the issues? That is a great precedent for the right and need of any assembly to evaluate and study the issues that bring conformity to godliness. Receiving the Word with enthusiasm and pursuing personal study that produces individual conviction is the best way to ensure openness to change.

Step A: Evaluation of the Church
The initial task is to understand the biblical imperatives given to the church so that the body can properly function. These imperatives and practices of the first-century church are used to evaluate the twentieth-century church. This process lasts about half a year and should include the following activities:

- Selection of an evaluation team
- Study and research
  - study of the biblical imperatives given to the church
  - exposure to biblically functioning churches

- Evaluation of the church's present philosophy and methodology
- Evaluation of the membership's perception of the ministry

Step B: Strategy for the Church

Based on the study of the biblical directives and practices, the evaluation team establishes the biblical philosophy for the church. A strategy for the implementation of that philosophy is determined (including Steps C–E) and developed. Certain activities should be performed during a six-month period:

- Development of a biblical philosophy of the church
- Development of a corresponding biblical methodology of the church
- Development of a strategy for change
  —study the extent of needed change
  —determine what changes must be made
  —study the impact of the changes
  —determine how the changes can best be made

PHASE TWO: LEADERSHIP DEVELOPMENT

During the second year, the church will begin to define different elements of a body of believers. These include biblical guidelines for leadership and the instruction and study necessary for directing ministry efforts.

Concerning leadership, a church may come to the conclusion that there are presently no men qualified according to 1 Timothy 3 or Titus 1 to serve as leaders in the church. That is not an insurmountable obstacle. The pattern in Antioch was, first, conversion and then later the appointment of elders (Acts 14:21–23). The time needed to develop leadership is a clear example of the fact that a church cannot fully function instantly.

If a church decides to consider bringing in leadership on the basis of recommendation or educational background, it should recognize that the basic principles of testing before serving would be strained (cf. 1 Tim. 3:10). That man should be considered temporary for at least a year, so that a relationship with the body can be established. Then either a more permanent commitment or satisfactory relocation arrangements can be made. Remembering that both the apostles and their official representatives (such as Timothy and Titus) served in unique and itinerant ministries

(2 Tim. 1:6; Titus 1:5), we recommend that the practice of importing outside shepherds to a flock should not be encouraged by an assembly.

Step C: Leadership Development

This period is considered an interim time. Questions of future leadership for the church are under initial consideration. Preferably current staff are sympathetic to the New Testament model and working towards similar goals. During these two years, the church body begins to see the work of Christian ministry more in terms of relationships and lives than a professional program conducted once a week.

Small group gatherings, following the pattern of the house churches in the New Testament, are to be considered an asset to the church. In these contexts believers can minister as individuals to other individuals in family and community contexts. The process of rethinking leadership and organization and meetings for the body is vital for transforming a church. There are methods a body can employ to accomplish their goal:

- Implementation of the biblical strategy
- Selection of potential leadership
  - manifestation of developing maturity
  - evidence of abilities for eldership
- Special teaching for potential leaders
  - instructional program during adult Sunday school
  - small group involvement on regular basis

PHASE THREE: DEVELOPING BIBLICAL ROOTS

Now the church is ready to begin to develop direction based on its study and experiences. Presuming that a number of men, qualified to lead, have surfaced and been recognized during this initial two years, each man is given a group of believers to oversee; this will become his shepherding group. These families and individual believers should be somewhat geographically near to one other and to him. The size of our homes naturally limits the size of these groups. We have found that an elder has a reasonably full ministry load with ten to twelve families and/or individuals from the body. As ministries develop and needs become known, we have found it is difficult for a man to handle many more. Of course, these shepherding groups are responsibilities that are additional to a man's vocation and family. If all elders are equal, and all are to shepherd the needs of the flock, it seems consistent that all have a shepherding group. This group becomes a prime support and encouragement for men in the ministry.

During this year the existing church body is divided into smaller groups for regular home meetings of study and fellowship. That is best accomplished with two guidelines: regularity of meeting and geographic distribution. Believers cannot know one another unless they meet together regularly in a context conducive to developing relationships. This is done with a recognition of community identity when the group members live relatively close and meet in one another's homes.

In the corporate church meeting, then, believers come together to praise the Lord for the growth in their individual lives and home meetings. They devote themselves to the New Testament priorities of the Word, the body of believers in fellowship, and prayer. Christian education is considered a primary responsibility of the parents, though the whole body of adult believers is responsible to minister to the children of the church as an extended family.

One small group program had gone from thirty-three groups to eighteen in less than a year and a half. This was the situation Ken faced when asked to come and "fix" a small-group Bible study program in a large church. It was a typical case study on how not to begin a program. Leaders had been selected and given a short course in discussion techniques, group dynamics, and Bible study. Then with fanfare and a festive sign-up evening, everyone in the church was encouraged to join the program that would provide what had been missing in the congregation—fellowship. The response was good—the result was tragic. Expectations were not fulfilled, leaders and participants became disillusioned and frustrated. When the smoke had cleared, almost half the groups no longer existed.

The mentality that demands everything be done instantaneously permeates the church to the extent that small groups have no chance to get off the ground. And church leaders—particularly those who stand in pulpits—say, "See, those small groups don't work!" No, they don't—if leadership is not developed and if the church does not understand the implications of, first, the responsibility of elders as pastor-teachers and, second, the responsibility of the church, under the elders, to function as a body. The transition of the local church to its proper role is crucial. Step C begins the process of developing the leadership; Step D provides the small group environment.

Step D: Shepherd Group Establishment

Step D focuses on the establishment of an ongoing program of the church in which the church is segmented by zones to eventually create an environment for mutual, reciprocal ministries under the leadership elders. This vital one-year plan includes the following:

- Establishment of shepherd groups
  - city is segmented into areas, or zones, that are assigned to individuals within that zone
  - initially two–three pilot groups are established; later the entire church is involved in a progressive manner
  - these groups are to continue indefinitely as they are incorporated into Step E
- Responsibility of shepherd group leadership
  - to begin to develop the leadership-flock relationships
  - to coordinate regular home meetings for study and fellowship
  - to provide pastoral ministry to the needs of his group
  - to begin to take part in management and ministry with church leadership

PHASE FOUR: DEVELOPING BIBLICAL FRUIT

As believers in the church begin to become known by the leadership of the church, they can be better encouraged in matters of discipleship and obedience to the commands of the Lord. From these men and women, leaders can be developed for the growing needs of the body. Shepherding groups are now established, and their numbers are growing. Elders from those groups are meeting together regularly for providing direction and oversight for the church.

Spiritual growth usually will produce numerical growth. What then? The answer is seen simply in the planting of daughter works in adjoining communities and in the preparation of sending leadership teams as missionaries to areas and cultures beyond the contacts of the community of the local church. The solution is not building bigger buildings.

How large is too large? We really do not know, but we have seen that as the assembly numbers in the multiple hundreds the challenges of knowing the flock, and ministering to it in a manageable fashion, becomes increasingly more difficult. The judgment of size is to be left up to each assembly, which has the same New Testament mandates to consider that we all do.

May we voice some cautions? First of all, we should be careful in citing the 3,000 of Acts 2. Not only was that a unique time of temporary residence associated with Pentecost, but the text carefully emphasizes that home meetings were held in conjunction with Temple meetings. Any kind of ministry that neglects or de-emphasizes the centrality of home or small group meetings is attempting something that is unrealistic for the church.

Second, the sheer numbers of multiple hundreds, if not thousands, of believers in an assembly demands both large buildings and elder boards that threaten to undo a church financially and logistically. We need to be extremely careful that we do not borrow the world's measuring stick of success here.

Step E: Establishing the Church According to the New Testament Model

This last step allows for the final basic remodeling of the church according to the New Testament guidelines to better accomplish the ministry mandates. Sufficient flexibility of staff, leadership, and ministry matters still exist to provide for the desires and insights of an assembly. No matter how strong and mature a body becomes, it cannot neglect certain matters:

- Final decisions are made concerning staff responsibilities and board of elders for the assembly. From this group could also come deacons and faithful men as well as women who begin to assume regular staff responsibilities to other women in the church.
- Shepherding groups are established under the leadership of the elders, while encouraging mutual ministries between believers.
- Necessary adjustments to the corporate meeting format and Christian education programs are made to come more closely in conformity to the New Testament model.

CONCLUSIONS

Talking to a brother about some of these principles of transition, with a format spread over a few years of church study and corporate commitment led to the following response. He just smiled and said, "Our church has undergone two splits in the last five years. Both of the fights have come over important matters: the first was over a name change, and the second was concerning Sunday school curriculum!" If that kind of observation were not typical, it might be humorous. But the fact is that churches do not historically change easily. The changes come in the context of a struggle that has caused believers to rethink the character and conduct of their church body. In more rare cases, churches have been encouraged in these changes by the mature and gentle teaching of resident pastoral staff.

Whatever the circumstances, and whatever the factors, modern theorists have never been able to improve on the New Testament model. It never becomes outdated. It never is in danger of obsolescence. It always has two supports that guarantee success:

> I will build my church, and the gates of Hades will not overcome it. (Matt. 16:18)
>
> For no one can lay any foundation other than the one already laid, which is Jesus Christ. (1 Cor. 3:11)

12

Beginning a New Church

Whether we are reading Scripture from the apostle Paul, the writings of Augustine or Luther, the sermons and instructions of Tauler or Spener, or the treatises of Warfield and Murray, the message is the same. The church is constantly subject to delusion and confusion. It needs skill, provided principally by its leadership, to reevaluate regularly its ministry efforts in light of the New Testament model.

Yet the subject of establishment of a new church, or church planting, most often is found in missions manuals. But the starting point for instructions on church planting is not through the school of missions but the discipline of biblical theology. For it is in theology and exegesis that we find our church planting bearings: in understanding the teachings of Christ to His disciples and in coupling the events of church growth in Acts with the ecclesiology of the epistles. Then, by understanding the character and mandates for the church, we are ready to evaluate that ministry process as it extends into communities where churches are needed.

Thus, steering a course that admittedly severs us from the moorings of convenience and convention, we launch into the subject of church planting—New Testament style.

WHERE DO WE START?

Determining a starting point for a new church is no easy matter. Some would say, "The need is in foreign fields. The vast majority of Christian ministry is in America; thus we are to be looking overseas." There is merit to that observation. We have already observed that the mandate of Matthew 28, called the Great Commission, presents the believer with a "going" posture with compassion for those who have not heard. This cannot be taken lightly.

Yet we had a saying in seminary: "If you go where there is need, you'll end up going everywhere." It is also true that there is a significant need for rethinking ministry here at home—in the context of neighborhoods and communities that have multiple religious activities and organizations, but still are much in need of consideration "in the inward travail of soul which the claims of truth demand." The task of spreading the truths that provide for proper conduct in the church remains to be applied with full energy to every tribe and country where opportunity exists.

FOUR CASE STUDIES

In the last ten years John has had the privilege of participating in the initial efforts and/or leadership of four local assemblies: two in Texas and two in Oregon. In each work he has learned new lessons, struggled with new challenges, and made his share of mistakes. But in each he has seen by the grace of the Lord the principles emphasized in this book bring spiritual growth and fruit. All four works today are ministering effectively in their communities.

In the first two churches in Texas, John was as much of an observer as a participant in the leadership process. He and his wife had the joy of teaching a small group of believers for about two years before they moved to Oregon. It was first in the sharing of life and experiences with those believers and those churches that they began to reevaluate what is to be the posture and priorities of a New Testament church.

After their move to Portland, they again became acquainted with a number of families who had similar desires. After a number of meetings and prayer sessions they started meeting in January 1977 in the gymnasium of a school. After one year the assembly moved its location, through merger with another small body of believers, to the current building where today the assembly still meets and fellowships together.

Their latest church planting effort began in fall 1980, recognizing a need for an assembly closer to their community. Having moved into the country, they requested from the Portland assembly permission to bring a leadership team, ourselves included, and interested members living near them into their community for the starting of this new church. They current church began through house meetings and then continued as they again found ourselves in the rented facilities of a public school.

The different matters under consideration in this chapter will be considered and illustrated in light of these new churches, which we hope will give more definite ideas for consideration in similar efforts. It might be that more light will come from our failures than from any successes that the Lord has given.

THE DILEMMA OF LOCATION

When considering starting a church in a community where evangelical churches already exist, the first step should never be the assumption that the community needs a new church. We must, rather, carefully evaluate and work with the believers and leadership of the established church bodies, attempting to bring renewal to them first. It is only after it becomes apparent that the community needs the ministry of a new church body—and this conviction is confirmed by other mature counsel—that plans and prayers can be made toward this end. We suggest the following advice: a person's commitment to a local church body should be firm and unswerving until the consistent practices of that assembly bring an individual believer's conscience into conflict with the truths of the New Testament concerning church ministry. Commitment to a church family is no light matter. Changes should be made only after careful thought and sincere prayer. Further, we feel an obligation to seek the discernment of pastors and leadership of existing churches in the community. We have yet to have a pastor discourage this kind of effort. If that had happened, we would have had to consider his concerns carefully.

Assuming that there is legitimate need for a new church in the community and that there is a consensus of leadership and families concerned with the ministry, then house meetings can begin. We recommend regular Sunday meetings while also developing the friendships and relationships through small groups. It is the norm to consider smallness a liability. In practice that just is not true; smallness is an advantage. It is only in the context of small groups and individual relationships that we can begin to know and love one another in the body of believers. Almost without exception, the first meetings in a home offer some of the best memories of ministry and fellowship for the families working in the initial planting effort. For some groups, the house church becomes the best, and final, answer to a community's need. If so, do not apologize for size of ministry.

We have also found that as the church grows in numbers, it may become necessary to arrange for rented public facilities. There are a number of reasons for that. First, it is not long before a typical home cannot facilitate the numerical needs of the church. Second, a public building allows a "neutral" setting for new members to consider the ministries of the assembly. Third, the facility brings in more leaders to guide the church and cultivate the lives of its young men for future leadership. Fourth, the building helps establish a core of believers who begin to make priorities in ministry that will lead to daughter works in adjacent communities and missions efforts overseas. The New Testament church was a blend of house churches and larger city churches, which combined the advantages of small group and larger group meetings (see chapter 7).

THE DEARTH OF LEADERSHIP

The first major challenge faced by the new church is the need for strong leadership. There are practical as well as technical reasons that is true. Practically, the needs of even a small group multiply quickly, and shepherds are needed to begin allocating substantial time to the needs of the church. Yet the abilities of a small group to financially support this shepherd, to some degree, are limited.

As well, there is a technical question of importance. In the New Testament we do not find men who ordain themselves. There is always a mother church and leadership from that church, or from the apostles, who set those men apart as elders to serve the needs of the assembly. But often for a new church there is not that sending or setting-apart agency. That awkwardness should not be minimized. Solutions are found, in part, in the ordained and confirmed resident or community Christian leadership—whether or not they are mother-church related.

Money matters. Given those initial concerns, the principal problems of leadership for a new church are in matters of support and ministry style. There are initial questions of whether leadership can, or should, be supported. Some believers will want missions to be the budget priority; others a building program. We always found sufficient challenge in paying the rent on a public facility. Money and ministry needs some clarification.

In the New Testament two principal groups were regularly supported. One group is familiar, the other is practically unknown. Both are seen in 1 Timothy 5:16–18:

> If any woman who is a believer has widows in her family, she should help them and not let the church be burdened with them, so that the church can help those widows who are really in need.
>
> The elders who direct the affairs of the church well are worthy of double honor, especially those whose work is preaching and teaching. For the Scripture says, "Do not muzzle the ox while it is treading out the grain," and "The worker deserves his wages."

Surprised? The New Testament church recognized by the time of the writing of this epistle the need to support two groups in the church: elders and qualified widows.

Concerning the widows, there are specific criteria. She must be clearly in need; without family who can help; aged; and a history of ministry in her community that is known by the church. The church has almost totally failed in that area. We have disregarded the needs and ministry contributions of our older saints. That pattern must be reversed if the household of God is to grow and prosper as it should.

The church was also to recognize the need to support its leaders. First Timothy 5:17 gave us some important guidelines (see chapter 8). Although all elders in an assembly are equal, the church is to recognize the need for, as much as possible, designating remuneration for elders who work hard at their ministries. Some leaders can function as staff resource elders who, being qualified due to their diligence, serve full-time because of the financial support of the church. Remember that these men are also shepherds and that they do not replace the other shepherds. All elders pastor the flock.

At one time in the Portland church, there were twelve elders, or pastors. Of the twelve, six men supported themselves in jobs and careers, three worked full-time, and the remaining three received part-time compensation in relation to diligence and need. But all twelve men had small-group responsibilities, since each elder is responsible for shepherding. In a different situation the distribution of ministry responsibilities could be spread differently between full-time, part-time, or non-compensated elders in the body.

These considerations bring up the related matter of compensation for men in vocational Christian ministries. In an extended section of Scripture from 1 Corinthians, Paul writes:

> If we have sown spiritual seed among you, is it too much if we reap a material harvest from you? If others have this right of support from you, shouldn't we have it all the more?
>
> But we did not use this right. On the contrary, we put up with anything rather than hinder the gospel of Christ. Don't you know that those who work in the temple get their food from the temple, and those who serve at the altar share in what is offered on the altar? In the same way, the Lord has commanded that those who preach the gospel should receive their living from the gospel.
>
> But I have not used any of these rights. And I am not writing this in the hope that you will do such things for me. I would rather die than have anyone deprive me of this boast. Yet when I preach the gospel, I cannot boast, for I am compelled to preach. Woe to me if I do not preach the gospel! If I preach voluntarily, I have a reward; if not voluntarily, I am simply discharging the trust committed to me. What then is my reward? Just this: that in preaching the gospel I may offer it free of charge, and so not make use of my rights in preaching it. (1 Cor. 9:11–18)

Notice the two equally valid principles that Paul carefully weaves through the text. The first principle of ministry support is that "the Lord has commanded that those who preach the gospel should receive their living from the gospel" (1 Cor. 9:14). Using the words of Christ, instruction from the Old Testament, and illustrations of the farm, Paul reminds the believers that men who labor in the ministry can reasonably expect to be supported by the ministry.

The second principle is equally clear. Paul was very concerned that the motives of a shepherd be above reproach. He chose not to receive support from those to whom he ministered. "But we did not use this right. . . . What then is my reward? Just this: that in preaching the gospel I may offer it free of charge, and so not make use of my rights in preaching it" (1 Cor. 9:12b, 18). Although there are reasonable rights for ministry support for men who labor in the ministry, it is equally legitimate to elect not to receive those funds. John has served with elders who gave both part- and full-time service to the church without compensation available to them. Of course, any funds not used for leadership support, for whatever reasons, can then be used in other areas of need.

Ministry perceptions. The second problem we have seen most regularly in new church ministries is more subtle but equally serious. It is concerned with ministry styles. In the first months, and even years, of a new church significant demands are felt by a church body. There are financial pressures, relational pressures, and endless demands on leadership from both within and outside the church. As the church develops its abilities to grow spiritually and thus meet the needs of other believers, the work usually grows numerically. As that happens, the church is responsible to progressively support its diligent elders to allow them the time necessary to serve.

Regardless of the teaching of the New Testament on multiple leadership one or more of the elders may think that the principle load of the ministry rests on his shoulders. That is a mistake. As a church grows numerically the elders will each be shepherding a small segment of the body, and the corporate worship will reflect the growth of those individual parts. Otherwise, numerical growth simply produces a large gathering without leaders who shepherd the flock. There is a need for wisdom and discipline in those matters in remembering that the ministry of a church is a responsibility shared and a ministry charged to a plurality of men in any local assembly. Depending on the format of the Sunday meeting, it is important that each elder provide teaching and leadership to the assembly. That models the truth of multiple ministry before the church and safeguards the flock from strange interpretations from any one man. Take note that Corinth had a multiple leadership model and the church was split by dissension and pride. Solutions are found in function as well as form.

WHERE ARE WE GOING?

After the initial obstacles of money and leadership styles are overcome, other considerations remain. Concerns over facilities, format, and community outreach are common. Establishment of regular home meetings and ministries to the men, the women, and the different age groups of the church are necessary in many cases. Certain additional observations may be helpful.

THE CHURCH IN COMMUNITY AND CELEBRATION

In the New Testament we find a careful emphasis on small group gatherings, as seen in the meetings of house churches, as well as special meetings for ministry problems (Acts 6:1–7), prayer (Acts 12:6–17), and disciplinary matters (1 Cor. 5:1–5). As the assembly of believers grew, there came larger churches, usually known as city churches, which provided for new ministry opportunities for members of the body. The two ministries provided the necessary balance of spiritual life for the church.

In any church there must be regular small group meetings. Those meetings in the homes of the saints provide contexts for relationships in the body and between the leadership and the assembly. That will lead to natural expressions of evangelism and outreach to neighbors and friends who would never consider "going to church." We have already seen in chapter 4 that this neighbor loving—as applied to believers and unbelievers—becomes the normal and natural context for church growth and evangelism (cf. Acts. 2:42–47).

The home meetings and the shepherding groups of the church provide contexts for the growth and development of the maturing saint. The gathered meetings on Sunday becomes the expression of that growth in individual lives expressed in corporate praise. A glimpse into this meeting is seen in 1 Corinthians:

> What then shall we say, brothers? When you come together, everyone has a hymn, or a word of instruction, a revelation, a tongue or an interpretation. All these must be done for the strengthening of the church. . . . But everything should be done in a fitting and orderly way (14:26, 40).

Apart from the questions of certain gifts for the church, notice the spirit and expectation of the New Testament body. As the believers gathered together, they came expecting to participate. We have already stated that there is no difference between laymen and clergy. We can also now say that all believers in the assembly are *ministers*. All are able and expected to participate in an orderly manner for the strengthening of the church.

In other words, if corporate expression is not allowed to take place in the body on a regular basis, then the church will not mature as it should. The careful balance between teaching and fellowship in small group meetings and corporate church life is vital for the church's health and growth.

ESTABLISHING MINISTRY CREDENTIALS FOR THE CHURCH

For a church formed to fulfill the guidelines of the New Testament model, certain temptations exist. They center on conforming to the expectations of either other churches in the area or the community at large. This conformity includes succumbing to looking for "church credentials" that fit traditional expectations. Essentially, these temptations take two forms: first, building up one man over another. This involves attaching the name of a man to a church (see chapter 8). That can be graciously resisted by affirming the truths of multiple leadership as well as the ministry responsibilities of a church as a body of believers.

The second temptation is just as apparent: building structures instead of people. It is the recognition that, almost universally, the church is seen as a physical plant more than a spiritual organism. Again, this temptation can be gently resisted. In our visitors' letter, we answer a number of typical questions raised about our church: "When are you planning to build?" Our answer: "We have no plans to build." In the Portland church, after a year, the Lord provided, without cost or debt, a large facility valued in excess of $500,000. They had just settled into enjoying the ministry on Sunday under the shadow of a gymnasium backboard. It is fine if the Lord provides a facility. But it is not worth pursuing as a necessary ministry goal. Building programs are certainly not worth church indebtedness; in some cases such funds absorb as much as fifty cents of every ministry dollar. Remember, the kingdom of God consists of spiritual more than physical matters (Rom. 14:17).

Ministry credentials are not established through corporate structures and institutions of brick and mortar. They are established by corporate growth and maturity. This is to be accomplished in a manner that proclaims Christ, and provides for the equipping of the saints for the work of service.

CONCLUSIONS

The Body of Christ, like its Model, should have two specialities. It should first specialize in truth. We want the claims of truth to be primary. We desire to avoid mental laziness, which lets conventional ideas dictate the course of the church. We want the ministries of the church to be measured according to the standard of the New Testament and the leadership to be responsible to the Chief Shepherd for the nurture and care of the flock.

But we also desire a second specialty: grace. We are to be men and women of grace, committed to a gentle spirit with those around us and a quiet but firm confidence in Christ. In any church planting effort both specialties must be valued as great priorities. Men and women must follow the dictates of the Word, their personal consciences, and the desire for community ministry.

13

Conclusion

Someone has said, "History makes liars of us all." The point, we believe, is that we are not good students of history. We seek to manage the challenges of our day without remembering that the same battles have been waged before and the same obstacles have been considered by the faithful who have lived before us.

On January 13, 1635, a baby boy was born in the village of Rappoltstein. He grew up in Strasbourg, learning the love of reading and the labor of ministry from his family and pastor.

This boy, Philip Jacob Spener, would become best known for his spiritual reform within the Lutheran church in Germany and in his writing of *Pia Desideria* ("Pious Desires"). The book became very popular until the traditionalists and the state clergy began to recognize the implications of its suggestions.

Spener urged reforms in the Lutheran church at ministry levels, following the model of the New Testament:

> This might be done, first of all, by diligent reading of the holy Scriptures, especially of the New Testament. It would not be difficult for every housefather to keep a Bible, or at least a New Testament, handy and read it every day or, if he cannot read, to have somebody else read.
>
> Then a second thing would be desirable in order to encourage people to read privately, namely, that where the practice can be introduced the books of the Bible be read one after another, at specified times in the public service.

For a third thing it would perhaps not be inexpedient to reintroduce the ancient and apostolic kind of church meetings. In addition to our customary services with preaching, other assemblies would also be held in the manner in which Paul describes them in 1 Cor. 14:26–40. Not a little benefit is to be hoped for from such an arrangement. Preachers would learn to know the members of their own congregations and their weakness or growth in doctrine and piety, and a bond of confidence would be established between preachers and people which would serve the best interests of both. In a short time they would experience personal growth and would be capable of giving better religious instruction to their children and servants at home."[1]

The priority of the Scriptures is there, the importance of the church meeting and regular participation in it, the need for relationships between "preacher" and people, and the transmission of that truth into the home. Whether it is Asia Minor in the first century, Germany in the seventeenth century, or America in the twentieth century, the need is the same. God's answer to the dilemma of man is Christ proclaimed, and believed, and lived out in the lives of His body, the church of the living God.

A few days before his death on February 5, 1705, Spener, known by some as "the spiritual counselor of Germany," gave instructions concerning his coffin:

During my life I have sufficiently lamented the condition of the church; now that I am about to enter the church triumphant, I wish to be buried in a white coffin as a sign I am dying in the hope of a better church on earth.[2]

The words of Christ and the apostles are similarly white. They are full of hope and confidence for the church. But that optimism is only as true as the blueprint behind it. The church is in need of a new restoration. The foundation remains the Lord Jesus Christ. The architects and builders are the church leadership. The blueprint is the New Testament. And the building is the Body of Christ.

In him the whole building is joined together and rises to become a holy temple in the Lord. And in him you too are being built together to become a dwelling in which God lives by his Spirit. (Eph. 2:21–22)

. . . I will build my church. (Matt. 16:18)

1. P. J. Spener, *Pia Desideria* (Philadelphia: Fortress Press, 1964), pp. 88–89.
2. Ibid., p. 24.

Moody Press, a ministry of the Moody Bible Institute, is designed for education, evangelization, and edification. If we may assist you in knowing more about Christ and the Christian life, please write us without obligation: Moody Press, c/o MLM, Chicago, IL 60610.